AN ECONOMIC MODEL OF THE MONEY MARKET IN THE UNITED STATES 1823-1859

This is a volume in the
Arno Press collection

Dissertations in American Economic History

Advisory Editor
Stuart Bruchey

Research Associate
Eleanor Bruchey

See last pages of this volume for a complete list of titles.

AN ECONOMIC MODEL OF THE MONEY MARKET IN THE UNITED STATES 1823-1859

Marie Elizabeth Sushka

ARNO PRESS
A New York Times Company
New York • 1978

Editorial Supervision: JOSEPH CELLINI

First publication in book form 1978 by Arno Press Inc.

DISSERTATIONS IN AMERICAN ECONOMIC HISTORY
ISBN for complete set: 0-405-11024-3
See last pages of this volume for titles.

Manufactured in the United States of America

Library of Congress Cataloging in Publication Data

Sushka, Marie Elizabeth.
An economic model of the money market in the United States, 1823-1859.

(Dissertations in American economic history)
Originally presented as the author's thesis, University of Georgia, 1974.
Bibliography: p.
1. Finance--United States--History. 2. Finance--United States--Mathematical models. 3. Money--United States--History. 4. Money--United States--Mathematical models. I. Title. II. Series.
HG181.S86 1978 332'.0973 77-14784
ISBN 0-405-11059-6

AN ECONOMIC MODEL OF THE MONEY MARKET IN THE UNITED STATES, 1823 - 1859

by

Marie Elizabeth Sushka

Assistant Professor of Economics

University of Georgia

For Myron B. Slovin who taught me about the search for knowledge and the love of truth

Table of Contents

List of Tables

List of Figures

Chapter 1

INTRODUCTION

This study has two basic objectives. First, contemporary monetary theory and econometric techniques are utilized in order to analyze the structure of the financial sector of the United States economy during the early 19th century. Such an approach provides an important test of whether the standard body of contemporary economic theory is capable of explaining a body of data generated by an economic environment distinctly different in character from the current economic conditions to which it is regularly applied. The results should indicate whether historical events must be analyzed as unique subjects, each requiring a different set of explanations, or instead can be viewed as new independent samples of data which are susceptible to the power of theoretical modeling and standard empirical techniques.

The second basic objective of this study is to determine whether the Bank War of the 1830's signifcantly altered or influenced the American financial structure.

The analysis is carried out within a neo-Keynesian framework. From the perspective of this body of theory, it is clear that if there were any economic effects of the Bank War, then they should be clearly observable in an analysis of the behavior of the financial sector. That is, if the failure to recharter the Second National Bank had any effect on the American economy as a whole, it must have been brought about through its effect on either the demand or the supply for financial assets. Any effects on the real economy through changes in the consumption or investment sectors, for example, would be indirect reactions to shifts in the financial market. Because of the limited degree of financial intermediation which characterized the pre-Civil War period, the problem of evaluating the effect of the Bank War on the financial sector can be confined to an examination of the money market, and more specifically, the behavior of the demand and supply for money.

The early 19th century was a period characterized by the specie flow mechanism and the absence of any effective governmental control over the money supply such as reserve requirements or open market operations. That is, the United States was a relatively open economy subject to fluctuations in the money supply through inflows and outflows of specie. Thus, since the monetary base was not set by government policy, any effect that the Bank War had on financial conditions must have occurred through shifts in either the public's demand for money, the commercial banking sector's willingness to supply liabilities, or both. Consequently, the estimation of these functions and an evaluation of their stability over the pre-Civil War period is the primary objective of this study.

Chapter 2

NEW PERSPECTIVES ON PAST RESEARCH

The Bank War has been examined at great length in American history. The roots of the debate about the economic impact of Jackson's failure to recharter the Second Bank of the United States reach far back, even into the 19th century. However, the object of this chapter is not to provide a detailed description of the numerous arguments and positions and their development over time. Instead, the literature on this topic is briefly but critically reviewed to show how economic analyses of the Bank War controversy have evolved and to indicate that this study is differentiated from previous research by its analytical approach and its use of econometric technique.

Previous research can be classified into two groups which use different methods of research and draw different conclusions. One group, the traditional school, concentrates on a subjective interpretation of events, personalities, and historical theses. The well known contributions of historians such as Hammond (29), Schlesinger (48), and Meyers (42) take this approach. Aside from their many specific ideas, these studies generally share the following basic conclusions: Jackson's failure to recharter the Second National Bank removed any effective restraint from the behavior of the commercial banking sector. Consequently, banks engaged in excessive note issue and speculative loan policies without proper specie backing. These so called wildcat banking practices intensified the speculation and inflation of the period. The situation was aggrevated by Jackson's economic policies particularly, the Specie Circular of 1836 which required payment in specie for all land purchases. The combination of these events culminated in the Panic of 1837.

The second group of researchers, the new or revisionist school, employs basic statistical tools in an attempt to analyze the Bank War empirically. This research has been undertaken by economists such as Stevens (53), Macesich (37), Rockoff (47), and especially Temin (56). Three basic conclusions characterize this group: The Bank War and Jackson's subsequent policies had no discernible economic effects. This is because the behavior of the commercial banking system was not affected by the removal of the federal authority vested in the Second National Bank. Furthermore, there are no indications of the existence of wildcat banking practices. Finally, the Panic of 1837 was precipitated by international events which were beyond domestic control.

The objective of this study is not to provide new hypotheses about the Bank War of the 1830's. Instead, contemporary monetary and macroeconomic theory and econometric techniques are used to analyze financial behavior during the early 19th century. Specifically, monetary theory is used to formulate models of the money market. Empirical specifications derived from these models are estimated by modern econometric techniques. Within this framework three hypotheses drawn from the literature of the traditional and new view are empirically tested. One, did the Bank War have any economic repercussions? Two, were wildcat banking practices characteristic of this period? Three, what were the causes of the Panic of 1837?

The approach taken by the traditional school is subjective in character and its methodology is not open to critical scientific examination even though its conclusions can be empirically tested. The second or new approach, although utilizing empirical information, does not use the theoretical models and sophisticated statistical methods of modern economics and has instead concentrated on analysis by inspection of data. However, because these researchers apply economic analysis to the problem, they are susceptible to criticism of how their analyses are formulated and empirical tools applied. There are two major criticisms of this work. First, the collection and reporting of data often lacks the degree of precision necessary for econometric techniques. For example, government statistics during the 19th century were collected on the basis of different fiscal years during different years. Prior to 1843, the government operated on a September based fiscal year, but in 1844 changed to a June basis. As a result, for one year government figures reflect only a six month rather than a twelve month period. However, this problem is typically ignored in the work of most of these researchers. Moreover, data are often compared which do not reflect the same reporting period so that a calendar year figure is inappropriately paired with a fiscal year figure. Differences in reporting periods are often a problem in modern analysis which is generally solved by applying interpolation techniques. This procedure, however, is not utilized in the Bank War literature.[1]

The second criticism is more basic. In contemporary monetary research a body of theory is applied in order to empirically estimate the underlying structure which generates the data. The economic structure is the economist's model of the behavior of the relevant institutions or groups and is the basis for interpreting events or drawing policy conclusions. The research on the Bank War by the new school, however, is not of this type. Instead, the analysis consists of inspection of the relevant data. There is no attempt at model building and, thus, no economic structure is estimated. Any empirical analysis is presented on an intuitive level only and generally consists of informal examination of ratios or indicies. This lack of model building and failure to estimate the parameters of the economic structure are unjustified, since there is both a large body of monetary theory and a relatively rich body of historical monetary data which can be effectively utilized for empirical testing. These problems are best illustrated in the work of Temin (56) who bases his conclusions on examination of various ratios or trends in a data series and ascribes to the relevant institutions a form of behavior which he believes is consistent with the data. A specific example is Temin's use of reserve ratios which are calculated in order to determine whether commercial bank behavior in the post Bank War period differed from the earlier period. Since the ratios are similar in both periods, Temin concludes that the failure to recharter the Second National Bank did not have any important economic effects. This conclusion, however, cannot be drawn directly from the data because the reserve ratio is an endogenous variable which must be functionally related to a variety of independent variables by means of a money supply function.[2] If the failure to recharter the Second Bank altered the financial behavior of either the commercial banking system or the public, the effects are embodied in the functional relationship and cannot generally be discerned in the data.

In general the approach of the traditional school is deficient because of its failure to explore the data relevant to its hypotheses. The problem with the research of the new school is its failure to analyze through use of the available data, the underlying behavioral functions implied by monetary theory and to use such a framework for testing relevant hypotheses. This study applies contemporary theory in order to specify the relevant behavioral functions to explain monetary affairs in the United States during the early nineteenth century. These functional relationships are estimated using standard empirical tools of econometrics and the available body of historical data. This approach provides specific quantitative evidence to test historical hypotheses about the impact of the Bank War.

The remainder of this study is organized as follows. The behavior of the demand and supply of money is examined in Chapter 3 and 4. The determinants of the public's demand for money are analyzed in Chapter 3. Several models of money demand are reviewed and the relevance for the pre-Civil War period assessed.

Empirical specifications are derived from these models and estimated separately for currency and bank liabilities. A similar treatment of the supply of money is provided in Chapter 4. Contemporary models of money supply are modified to take account of the institutional arrangements which characterized the Bank War period. The empirical specifications derived from these models are tested and the results analyzed. Both the demand and supply of money equations are estimated over the sample period 1823-1859 using annual data. The stability of the demand and supply of money functions is investigated in Chapter 5. This is done by splitting the full sample into two sub-periods and estimating separate equations. This procedure provides evidence about the pattern of the estimated coefficients over time and provides a framework for evaluating the major hypotheses about the economic impact of the Bank War. Conclusions are drawn in Chapter 6.

Chapter 3

THE DEMAND FOR MONEY

3.1 Theoretical Development

The subject of money demand lies at the heart of monetary economics. Consequently, it has been analyzed both theoretically and empirically more than any other subject in the field of monetary behavior. Although the origins of the subject can be traced back to the classical model, there has actually been little divergence as to what are the appropriate determinants of money demand. In almost every study the quantity of money demanded is assumed to be a function of income and interest rates. The voluminous literature which has developed on the subject is in fact primarily directed to rationalizing these determinants and analyzing their quantitative importance.[1]

The basic work on the demand for money was originated by the classical or quantity school which first articulated the transactions motive for holding money.[2] It was assumed that the need for money balances arises because of the inherent lack of synchronization between receipts and expenditures. The key concept is an identity which describes the transactions velocity of the circulation of money:

$$MV = PT \tag{3.1}$$

where M is the quantity of money, V is the velocity or number of times money turns over, P is the price level and T is the volume of transactions. In this relationship the supply of money is assumed to be exogenously determined as is the volume of transactions. Velocity, the ratio of the volume of transactions to the money supply is considered to be a constant established by technical considerations. Consequently, in this model prices are the only endogenously determined variable, varying with the supply of money. Thus the demand for money balances is viewed as a constant fraction of the value of transactions, written as:

$$M_d = kPT \qquad \text{where } k = \frac{1}{V}. \tag{3.2}$$

The primary contribution to money demand theory of the classical school is that holdings of money balances are maintained in order to fulfill transactions requirements. Since transactions are assumed to be a constant proportion of national income, the demand for money is viewed as a simple function of national income. It is important to note that in the classical theory, the rate of interest plays no role in either the demand or the supply of money. Instead, it is the equilibrating mechanism in the savings and investment market.

The link between the classical school and the Keynesian contributions to the theory of money demand was provided by the Cambridge economists. This school hypothesized that an individual holding money for transactions purposes is aware of the opportunity cost of holding money balances. This cost is the rate of interest that is earned on alternative assets that are close substitutes for money. The volume of transactions is still considered to be a stable proportion of the level of income or wealth but, the velocity of money, the ratio of income to money, is considered a function of alternative interest rates. Thus the Cambridge version of the classical quantity theory of money utilized the same equation of exchange

$$M_d = kPY \qquad (3.3)$$

but with Y, national income, replacing physical transactions and k, the inverse of velocity, no longer a constant but instead a parameter which varies with the level of interest rates or expectations.[3]

The Keynesian theory of money demand represented a

major extension of the model developed by the Cambridge school. Keynes specified three motives for the holding of money balances: the transactions motive, the precautionary motive, and the speculative motive.[4] Keynes analyzed the first two motives jointly and considered them simple functions of income. He also hypothesized a speculative demand for money which varied inversely with the interest rate on bonds. In Keynes' view, when the interest rate on bonds is low, investors expect a rise in yields which entails capital losses. Consequently, low interest rates induce the public to hold substantial speculative balances. Alternately when interest rates are high, speculative holdings of money are low since investors desire to maintain substantial bond holdings in order to earn capital gains when interest rates eventually fall. Thus Keynes suggested that overall, the holding of money balances is strongly interest elastic.

It should be noted that in the Keynesian analysis the only alternatives available to investors are money or bonds. Thus, the Keynesian model is probably the most appropriate framework for analyzing the demand for money in the pre- Civil War period which is characterized by an absence of a wide variety of secure financial instruments, and by relatively thin capital markets for those which did exist.[5] Overall the Keyneisan model suggests that in the pre-Civil War period money balances should vary positively with income and negatively with the bond rate.

In the contemporary period financial markets are characterized by a substantial variety of riskless assets which are substitutes for money. Recent neo-Keynesian theory derives the interest elasticity of money demand from optimal inventory and portfolio diversification models. Thus, Keynes' results are justified without accepting the validity of his restrictive assumptions about capital market behavior. However, because the Keynesian assumptions are so applicable to the pre-Civil War period and since these models imply essentially the same empirical specifications as Keynesian theory, this modern theoretical work will not be analyzed here.[6]

In general the theory of money demand suggests that demand for money balances can be specified as

$$M_d = k(i)Y \qquad \frac{\partial k}{\partial i} < 0 \tag{3.4}$$

where M_d is money balances and Y is nominal gross national product. The k(i) represents an array of interest rates which reflect the opportunity cost of holding money where money holding and the interest rate are assumed to be negatively related. In the empirical work on money demand it is standard to modify equation (3.4) by taking logarithms of both sides of the equation so that the function becomes

$$\ln M_d = \ln k(i) + \ln Y \qquad (3.5)$$

which is linear in logarithms and has constant elasticities. The velocity variable k(i) is considered to be a function of interest rates on assets that are close substitutes for money and is approximated by a set of these yields, assumed to be linear in logarithms. This is the basic model of money demand that is tested in the empirical work in this study. This model, referred to as Model I, is modified in three ways in order to provide alternative specifications for empirical testing.

The second model modifies the specifications of equation (3.5) to allow for partial adjustment to equilibrium.[7] Model II is drawn from the Pigou-Latané formulation that

$$M^* = k(i)Y \qquad \frac{\partial k}{\partial i} < 0 \qquad (3.6)$$

where M* is desired money balances. It is hypothesized that actual money demand, M, adjusts only gradually to the desired amount so that

$$\Delta M = \lambda(M^* - M_{-1})$$

$$= \lambda(k(i)Y - M_{-1}) \quad (3.7)$$

Rewriting equation (3.7) in logarithmic form yields

$$\ln M - \ln M_{-1} = \lambda(\ln M^* - \ln M_{-1})$$

$$= \lambda(\ln k(i) + \ln Y - \ln M_{-1}) \quad (3.8)$$

where λ is the speed of adjustment, which indicates the proportion of adjustment that occurs in one period. Solving for M yields the specification for empirical testing:

$$\ln M = \lambda \ln k(i) + \lambda \ln Y + (1-\lambda)(\ln M_{-1}) \quad (3.9)$$

An alternative specification of this approach, Model III, is obtained by subtracting the logarithm of national income from both sides of equation (3.9) so that

$$\ln M - \ln Y = \lambda \ln k(i) + (1-\lambda)(\ln M_{-1} - \ln Y) \quad (3.10)$$

This procedure is equivalent to constraining the income elasticity to be unity.[8] Use of such a constraint permits more effective estimation of the remaining parameters[9] particularly because ofthe serious multicollinearity which is usually present between interest rates and income. The validity and usefulness of this procedure depends on whether the constraint is valid.

In the last specification, Model IV, a refinement about price expectations is incorporated into the three previous models. The importance of price expectations in analyses of money demand has been a basic tenet in the views of the modern quantity theorists.[10] Briefly, the quantity theorists as typified by the work of Friedman (18), postulate that money is a commodity which yields a flow of services and can be treated as a good in consumer demand theory. Thus, the more money held, the less valuable its services relative to the services of other assets. Moreover, the relevant opportunity costs for money are the rates of return obtained by holding assets other than money. Quantity theorists allow for substitution between real assets and money holdings so that in addition to bond rates the yields on equities, durable goods and human capital are relevant opportunity costs. The inflation rate is viewed as the rate of return on real assets and consequently when the rate of inflation is expected to rise, it is assumed that the public will substitute out of money holdings and into real assets. Quantity theorists also suggest that the ratio of human to non-human capital may influence the demand for money, since the higher the human component, the greater the demand for money to compensate for the lack of marketability of human capital.

In general, the modern quantity theorists suggest that the demand for money should be a function of wealth, the yield on bonds, the rate of inflation, and the ratio of human to non-human wealth. In the empirical formulation, Friedman (17) actually specifies money holdings as a function of bond yields, inflation, and permanent income. The primary difference between this view and the Keynesian theory is that in Keynesian analysis substitution out of money holdings into real assets is considered unrealistic and only substitution between closely related assets is considered; typically, bonds are assumed to be the close substitute for money holdings. In order to test for the presence of substitution between money and real assets, the change in the price level in logarithmic terms is added to each of the previous specifications since it is assumed that price expectations must be related to observed price changes.

If such a pattern of substitution is present, the price variable should take on a negative sign. It should be noted however, that modern empirical work including that of Friedman (17) has consistently failed to find any impact of the rate of change of prices on the demand for money.

3.2 Empirical Evidence: Preliminary Considerations

The four theoretical models developed previously are subjected to empirical testing over the sample period 1823 through 1859 using yearly data. The Second National Bank began operations in 1817; however, the 1823 starting point is used in the empirical tests for several reasons.

The primary reason for this choice of sample period is that the Bank's policies differed significantly between the periods 1817-1822 and 1823-1836. During the first several years of operation, the two successive presidents of the Bank engaged in self-defeating as well as contradictory policies. The first president, William Jones, in office from 1817 to 1819, a post war period characterized by speculation and inflation, carried out highly speculative credit expansion policies which were in violation of the national charter. Bank stock illegally bought on margin by Bank officers for purposes of speculation, represented a considerable portion of total Bank loans. Furthermore, overexpansion of note circulation, based on illiquid long term loans made by the branches of the Bank in the South and West, brought about heavy pressure on the specie reserves of the parent

Bank where most redemption of notes occurred. Moreover, the Bank failed to pursue any rigorous policy of specie redemption of state notes which might have curtailed note expansion and lessened the pressure on specie reserves. Thus by 1818 the Bank whose major purpose had been to restore financial order by assuring the convertibility of bank notes into specie had seriously overextended its credits and in particular added to the speculation in land. By 1819 several branches of the Bank failed and Jones resigned. Langdon Cheves, a strong administrator, succeeded Jones and held office from 1819-1822. He replaced the expansionary policies of Jones with sharply contractionary policies. He instituted a severe credit deflation and liquidation of Bank assets by redeeming in specie both state and branch notes and foreclosing all unpaid loans. The panic of 1819 and the succeeding years of deflation marked the Cheves administration which lasted through 1822. Subsequent to these events, Nicholas Biddle took over the Bank as president in 1823 and remained in that position for the duration of the Bank's charter. It was Biddle who pursued innovative policies in an attempt to make the Bank an effective central bank in fiscal matters as well as in controlling the money supply, managing foreign exchanges and investment practices, and conducting discount business. Consequently, the initial years of the Bank's existence are omitted so that the observations form a sample period characterized by relatively consistent and straightforward financial policies.

An additional reason for eliminating the period 1817-1822 is the serious problems with the data.[11] The elimination of such a period from the sample presents no econometric problems. However, very deleterious effects result from including a number of observations which are drawn from a population different than that of the remaining sample. Thus, it is usually the case that data known to be suspicious, a priori, are excluded.[12]

Most of the theoretical and empirical work in the literature on money demand is formulated in aggregate terms. That is, the dependent variable is usually taken to be M1, defined as demand deposits plus currency, or M2, defined as commercial bank time deposits plus M1. In fact, a substantial amount of work in money demand has been directed in large part to the issue of which monetary aggregate measure is the more appropriate dependent variable.[13] However, very recent contemporary work has taken the direction of disaggregating money holdings into currency and some measure of bank liabilities and estimating each variable separately based on specifications derived from standard money demand theory.[14]

There are several reasons for this disaggregation. First, the quantities of currency and bank liabilities are determined by different economic processes within an economic model. The quantity of currency held by the public is determined solely by public demand. However, the quantity of bank liabilities outstanding results from the interaction of the public's demand for these liabilities and the willingness of the commercial banks to supply them through adjustments in their portfolio holdings. Second, the disaggregation of bank liabilities and currency is also justified on the grounds that the public considers the two categories of financial assets to be different despite the large degree of substitution between them.[15] For example, while currency is usually more acceptible than bank liabilities as a means of payment, there is a greater degree of risk or loss or theft. In particular, it is also typical that service costs are associated with the holding of demand deposits but not currency.

The reasons for differentiating between the

components of the money supply are especially important within the context of the early 19th century. At that time, currency consisted of both minted and unminted specie which was a consistently marketable store of value. However, bank liabilities, defined as demand deposits plus notes, were subject to wide geographical divergence in their rates of interest and discount. Thus, although there was always a considerable risk of loss or theft associated with the holding of currency while bank liabilities were relatively secure, currency circulated at face value whereas bank liabilities were often accepted only at a discount.

Consequently, it is reasonable to expect that the demand for demand deposits plus bank notes might be characterized by a separate functional relationship from that of the demand for currency, especially in view of the circumstances which prevailed in the early 1800's. That is, these dependent variables can be expected to differ with regard to their income or interest rate elasticities and perhaps their speeds of adjustment toward equilibrium. Consequently in this study, regressions for money demand are estimated separately for bank liabilities and currency.[16]

3.3 The Demand for Bank Liabilities

The regressions for the demand for commercial bank liabilities are found in Table 3.1. The regressions are estimated using ordinary least squares. However, when the presence of excessive positive serial correlation in the residuals is observed as indicated by a low Durbin-Watson statistic, the regression is reestimated using a first-order autoregressive technique.[17] The t statistics appear in parentheses below the coefficients in the table.[18] The variables specified in these regressions follow from the theoretical models developed previously. Both bank liabilities and income[19] are in nominal terms.[20] All reported equations are in logarithmic form and therefore coefficients are in fact the elasticities of the variables. Interest rates on three financial instruments which might be effective substitutes for money are used in order to approximate k(i) in the theoretical formulations: the long term government bond rate, RL[21]; the municipal bond rate, RMUN; and the commercial paper rate RCP[22].

It might be useful to note that the character of the markets differed for these three instruments during the pre-Civil War period. As Homer(31), Myers (71), and Davis (12) have noted, a well organized market for commercial paper

Table 3.1

Demand for Bank Liabilities; Logarithmic Form , 1823-1859

Dependent Variable	Y	RL	RMUN	RCP	DUM
1) MD	.8360 (5.98)	-1.2126 (-3.30)			
2) MD	.8740 (5.34)		-.0573 (-.06)		
3) MD	.7815 (4.10)			-.0948 (-1.27)	.3548 (1.68)
4) MD	.3932 (3.55)	-.7253 (-2.94)			
5) MD/Y		-1.1766 (-3.20)			
6) MD/Y		-.7110 (-2.90)			
7) MD	.8365 (6.25)	-1.1990 (-3.28)			
8) MD	.4236 (3.73)	-.6899 (-2.78)			
9) MD/Y		-1.1652 (-3.18)			
10) MD/Y		-.6777 (-2.74)			

Table 3.1

(continued)

	Lagged Dependent Variable	PDOT	Constant	R^2/SE	DW/Rho
1)			2.7671	.93	1.97
			(2.85)	.133	.69
2)			.7913	.91	2.01
			(.46)	.153	.70
3)			1.0647	.91	1.88
			(1.08)	.150	.74
4)	.5689		1.3499	.92	1.80
	(5.20)		(2.88)	.139	
5)			1.8433	.61	1.96
			(3.23)	.134	.69
6)	.5851		1.1315	.58	1.80
	(5.48)		(3.00)	.138	
7)		.2772	2.7426	.93	2.06
		(1.03)	(2.92)	.133	.68
8)	.5294	.4011	1.3422	.92	1.92
	(4.63)	(1.13)	(2.88)	.139	
9)		.2603	1.8261	.61	2.04
		(.96)	(3.21)	.134	.68
10)	.5546	.3439	1.0801	.58	1.90
	(4.93)	(.98)	(2.84)	.138	

did not exist before the Civil War. Instead, most borrowers relied on personal banking connections. In fact, no data on commercial paper rates exist for the period prior to 1831 and the data available for the period 1831-1859 are characterized by extraordinary volatility. The market for bonds, however, was much more efficiently organized. Payne and Davis (44) indicate that during the pre-Civil War period an institutional market existed for federal as well as state and municipal bonds which allowed an investor to buy and sell bonds quickly and easily. Myers (71) indicates that prices for these bonds were quoted daily in New York and Cole (72) reports that these quotations were reproduced in local newspapers throughout the eastern states. Furthermore, Cole finds that substantial regional financial interrelationships existed which centered on the New York market. In fact, Cole reports a monthly index for prices on high quality long term securities beginning in 1802 and Homer reports a yearly series for the yield on long term federal government bonds. Thus, although the American capital market was in general not well developed by contemporary standards, investors did have access to sound and readily marketable long term securities.

The first three equations in Table 3.1 are the empirical results obtained by using Model I in which the level of bank liabilities is specified as a function of income and interest rates. In each equation the income elasticity is high, between .78 and .87, and quite significant. In fact, these elasticities differ from unity by only one standard error.[23] Initially combinations of these three primary interest rates were included in one regression. However, the problem of the multicollinearity endemic to interest rate data on a time series basis prohibited any effective estimation of the interest rate effects or any clear interpretation of the results. Consequently each rate is entered in a regression separately in order to clarify the individual effects. The long term interest rate, RL, in equation (1) is significantly negative with a high elasticity of -1.2. The municipal bond rate, in equation (2), has the correct negative sign but the elasticity is very small and has no statistical significance. The commercial paper rate, in equation (3), also obtains the correct negative sign but is not statistically significant. Each of these three interest rates are used throughout the empirical testing of the money demand models. However, throughout the results both RMUN and RCP uniformly fail to obtain a significant coefficient and consequently, only the regression results for the government bond rate are analyzed.

The statistical properties of equation (1) are extremely good. In addition to the reasonable elasticities obtained for the income and interest rate variables both of which are quite significant, the degree of explanation is a rather high 93 percent. The standard error is low and the rho coefficient is only .69 which is not high for time series data. Thus, it can be concluded that the standard theory of money demand explains rather well the behavior of the demand for money in the pre-Civil War period.

Equation (4) reports the empirical results of applying Model II which allows for a gradual adjustment of desired to actual money holdings. The speed of adjustment indicated by this equation is about 43 percent per year which is close to the results implied by modern money equations estimated on quarterly data.[24] The short run income elasticity is about .40 and is highly significant. The long run income elasticity implied by the equation is about .91[25] which is again only one standard error away from unity and closely parallels the initial results contained in equation (1). The short term interest rate elasticity in equation (4) is about .72 which again is significant. The implied long run interest rate elasticity is quite strong, about -1.68. The goodness of fit of the equation remains quite high as indicated by the high R^2 and low standard error statistics.

Nevertheless, it should be noted that the statistical properties of equations with lagged dependent variables are often suspect. As Griliches (28) and others have demonstrated, the problem is that lagged dependent variables often capture the serial correlation of the residuals rather than providing any information about the dynamic behavior of the dependent variable. Equation (4) suggests the presence of this phenomenon inasmuch as it has a high Durbin-Watson statistic and does not require an adjustment for serial correlation which is needed in equation (1). In order to provide some additional information about this question, a specification is estimated with money demand explained by both current and lagged income. If substantial lags exist in the behavior of money demand as implied by equation (4), it should become apparent in estimating such an equation. The results are reported below:

$$\ln MD = \underset{(1.91)}{.656} \ln Y + \underset{(.71)}{.25} \ln Y_{-1} + \underset{(.62)}{.548} + .70u_{-1}$$

$$R^2 = .91 \qquad S.E.=.152 \qquad D.W.=1.16$$

The estimation results do not provide any indication of serious lags in money demand behavior and thus the results of equation (4) must be regarded with caution. It is, however, reassuring to note that the steady state properties of equation (4) are almost identical to the results obtained by specifying only income and interest rates, equation (1).

Because the long run income elasticity in equations (1) and (4) is close to unity, it is appropriate to apply an alternate specification, Model II, in which the elasticity of income is a priori constrained to unity. The results are reported as equations (5) and (6). In equation (5) the only explanatory variable is RL which has an elasticity of -1.18 and a t statistic in excess of 3. The R^2 in this equation is .61 but cannot really be compared with the previous R^2s because the dependent variables are different. Instead, the standard error statistic should be used for purposes of comparison. The standard error of equation (5) is about .134 which is essentially the same as that of equation (1). In equation (6) the lagged dependent variable is added to the specification. The calculated speed of adjustment is about .42 which is slightly slower than in equation (4). The interest rate variable is strongly significant and quite large with a long run elasticity of about -1.71. Although the R^2 is low, the standard error is approximately the same size as in the previous regressions.

Overall, these results are strikingly similar and indicate general robustness of the specifications. Each equation implies an income elasticity that is quite large and fairly close to unity,even when a lagged dependent variable is included. The long term interest rate, RL, in each specification obtains a large and significant elasticity in the range of -1.2 to-1.7. The speed of adjustment is consistently reasonable in magnitude, about 40 percent per year. All six equations fit well and have low standard errors.

The remaining four equations, (7) - (10) in Table 3.1, incorporate a price expectations variable, PDOT, into each of the previous specifications. The results are consistently poor. The PDOT variable fails to have the correct negative sign and is not significant.[26] In view of the insignificant results for PDOT, it is not surprising that the coefficients of the other variables remain essentially unaffected.

In general the robustness of contemporary monetary theory is evident in the empirical results for the early 19th century. This indicates that the public's demand for bank liabilities during the period 1823-1859 increased almost proportionately with increases in income and was very sensitive to changes in interest rates. Furthermore the results indicate that, despite the sometimes extreme fluctuations in prices over this period, the public's demand for money was not sensitive to the rate of price change. These findings also indicate that the public's demand for money was robust throughout the period of the Bank War. On this basis there is no indication that the demand side of the money market was in any way disturbed by the Bank War of the 1830's. However, these results alone are not sufficient evidence to warrant the conclusion that money demand was not affected by the Bank War. Instead, the structural stability of these equations must be analyzed by examining the pattern of the coefficients which result when specifications are reestimated over various subperiods of the sample. Consideration of this problem is postponed until the behavior of the supply of money is investigated.

3.4 The Demand for Currency

In this section the behavior of the demand for currency is empirically investigated. The results are reported in Table 3.2. Since the ordinary least square estimation was characterized by a high degree of serial correlation in the residuals only the results obtained by applying the Cochrane-Orcutt autoregressive technique are reported in the table. The variables are again in nominal terms and all equations are estimated in logarithmic form. The interest rate variables used in this analysis are the same as those employed in the estimation of the equations for bank liabilities.

Although the same theoretical model of money demand is applied to the demand for currency, it can be hypothesized that the empirical results may differ, particularly with respect to the size of the income and interest rate elasticities. The empirical findings typical of the contemporary literature suggest that the income elasticity of currency is expected to be smaller or, at most, the same size as that of bank liabilities.[27] The usual reason is that currency is primarily utilized for small consumer expenditures

Table 3.2

Demand for Currency; Logarithmic Form , 1823-1859

	Y	RL	RMUN	RCP	DUM	Lagged Dependent Variable	Constant	R^2/SE	DW/Rho
1) MC	2.2451 (14.26)	.5999 (1.13)					-8.6672 (-7.25)	.97 .202	1.48 .58
2) MC	2.1211 (14.40)		3.2993 (2.70)				-12.3600 (-6.62)	.97 .187	1.65 .56
3) MC	2.1531 (11.72)			.0592 (.55)	.0577 (.20)		-7.4092 (-8.27)	.97 .205	1.55 .57
4) MC	2.2329 (3.06)						-7.6808 (-9.12)	.97 .202	1.53 .58
5) MC	.7104 (3.06)					.7068 (7.07)	-2.4814 (-2.96)	.98 .156	1.64 .13
6) MC/Y		.3986 (.34)					-1.8512 (-1.01)	.00 .699	.07
7) MC/Y		.1380 (.45)				.9840 (21.85)	-.1622 (-.34)	.94 .174	1.50 .05

which typically form a smaller and smaller proportion of income as income increases. Similarly there is a general consensus in the literature that the interest elasticity of currency should be of lesser importance than that of bank liabilities.[28] This is because most consumer holdings of currency are small so that substitution into interest bearing instruments involves prohibitive transactions costs, especially in terms of time and effort, relative to the potential return available.

The results of applying the standard theory, Model I, in which currency is specified as a function of income and interest rates, are reported as equations (1)-(3). In each equation the interest rate variable obtains an incorrect, positive sign. Consequently, there is no evidence of any degree of substitution between currency and interest bearing assets. The results are not surprising and are consistent with the contemporary literature. Furthermore, the income elasticities in equations (1)- (3) are estimated to be quite large, exceeding two, with t ratios in excess of eleven. When income is specified without including an interest rate variable,as reported in equation (4), a similar result is obtained. The goodness of fit is quite high with over 97 percent of the variation in the dependent variable explained and with a low standard error statistic.

The results for the income variable, however, differ substantially from those found in the contemporary literature , since the estimate of the income elasticity of currency demand is more than twice that of the demand for bank liabilities. The power of this result is demonstrated by estimating Model II where the income elasticity is constrained to unity, as reported in equation (6). The serious degree of this misspecification is indicated by the sharp rise of the standard error to almost .70. This clearly suggests that constraining this elasticity to unity is not appropriate. When a lagged dependent variable is added, equation (7), it obtains a coefficient of .99 which suggests that currency demand adjusts toward equilibrium at one percent per year. This is clearly not sensible and can be ascribed to the misspecification induced by applying an inappropriate constraint.

The size of the income elasticity results, however, are reasonable when viewed within the framework of early 19th century financial conditions. Modern analyses assume that bank liabilities are a more desirable asset than currency which is held only because certain consumer transactions are not well suited to payment by check. Thus, a rise in income induces a greater percentage increase in the holdings of bank liabilities than currency. During the early 1800's, however, specie was accepted at face value and thus was probably more desirable for many purposes than bank liabilities which were constantly subjected to widely fluctuating discount rates. Thus it can be concluded that the empirical results provide evidence as to how strong this preference for currency was during the period.

The estimation results obtained when the currency demand specification allows for gradual adjustment toward equilibrium are shown in equation (5). The estimated speed of adjustment is about 30 percent per year which is fairly slow. The steady state effect of income on currency, however, is almost exactly that obtained in equations (1) through (4). Thus once again, it is quite likely that the lagged dependent variable captures the effect of the serial correlation in the residuals rather than any real dynamics in the behavior of currency demand. Consequently, these results must be treated with caution. Equation (4) remains the preferable specification.

Overall as in the case of bank liabilities the empirical results for currency demand emphasize the robustness and power of contemporary theoretical and empirical financial models in explaining early 19th century behavior. Although money demand theory specifies an interest rate elasticity as a determinant of demand, modern empirical evidence suggests that such a variable should play only a small role in currency behavior. In this respect, the evidence reported in this study is consistent with modern results. In general, the demand for currency is primarily a function of movements in income with an elasticity greater than two.

In summary, the empirical tests of the demand for bank liabilities and the demand for currency provide important evidence on the basic questions set forth at the beginning of this study. First, all the evidence indicates that the standard body of contemporary monetary theory is capable of explaining the behavior of the demand side of the financial sector of the United States economy during the early 1800's. Second, the results obtained are quite robust and have an extremely high degree of explanatory power. Third, there is no obvious indication, thus far, that the Bank War of the 1830's either altered or influenced the pattern of demand for financial instruments within the American financial structure. This implies that Jackson's policies towards the Second National Bank did not induce the severe economic fluctuations of the post Bank period. A more thorough analysis of this question, however, is postponed until the behavior of the supply of money is analyzed.

Chapter 4

THE SUPPLY OF MONEY

4.1 Theoretical Development

In the last decade monetary economics has developed a behaviorialistic treatment of the commercial banking system. This implies that within the framework of monetary theory the supply of money is an endogenously determined variable. Prior to this development, commercial bank behavior was considered to be mechanical. The older view is still found in many standard textbooks of money and banking. It implies that the Federal Reserve controls the money supply through alterations in bank reserves, which are then multiplied by the inverse of the reserve ratio as banks "create" money from the inflow in reserves. The process of monetary expansion is initiated ,for example, by a purchase of government securities by the Federal Reserve System which increases the cash assets of the selling bank by an amount equal to the sale. This amount is loaned out by the bank and eventually returns as deposits to the banking system. After meeting deposit reserve requirements, the banks again loan out the remaining funds. Eventually, the full amount of the open market sale becomes part of bank reserves, with the overall increase in the money supply equal to the value of the sale divided by the reserve ratio. This description implies that the money supply can be viewed as an exogenous variable controlled by the Federal Reserve. Thus, the central bank sets the money supply and the interest rate in the demand for money function adjusts to equate demand and supply. In this system it is demand which adjusts to exogenously determined supply. The applicability of this simplistic view of the money supply mechanism, however, is not easily rationalized for the conditions of the early 19th century. First, no institution at that time controlled the stock of high powered money. Second, there were no uniform, legal reserve requirements on deposits to automatically limit the degree of expansion in the money supply induced by an inflow of specie reserves.[1]

Current theory on the supply of money is more applicable to early 19th century America and thus this version of the determinants of the money supply is reviewed here. According to this theory, the money supply is considered to be endogenously determined by the interaction of public demand and bank portfolio adjustment. First, it is assumed that the total amount of high powered money, currency plus bank reserves, is exogenously determined, that is independent of present monetary conditions. Second, it is assumed that commercial banks behave in a manner consistent with profit maximization. That is, commercial banks adjust their asset portfolios in response to changes in the yields on financial instruments. Consequently, the quantity of actualreserves maintained by banks varies.

In contemporary literature, the money supply is derived as follows. First, total reserves at commercial banks are defined as

$$TR = UR + BR \tag{4.1}$$

where UR is unborrowed reserves and BR is borrowed reserves. But unborrowed reserves are defined as the sum of required reserves, RR, plus the difference between excess, ER, and borrowed reserves

$$UR = RR + ER - BR \, . \tag{4.2}$$

By definition

$$FR = ER - BR \tag{4.3}$$

where FR is free reserves, and

$$RR = z_D\ MD, \tag{4.4}$$

where z_D is the reserve requirement on demand deposits, MD.[2] That is, required reserves are those holdings of deposits at the Federal Reserve plus vault cash which the banks must legally maintain to support the current level of deposit liabilities. Substituting equations (4.3)and (4.4) into (4.2) the following expression is obtained:

$$UR = z_D MD + FR. \tag{4.5}$$

Rearranging term yields

$$MD_s = \frac{UR - FR}{z_D} \tag{4.6}$$

which is the identity for the supply of money.

Within this identity, free reserves are assumed to be endogenous and a function of market interest rates, i, and the discount rate, d, at which banks can borrow[3] so that

$$FR = FR\ (i,d)\ \frac{\partial FR}{\partial i} < 0, \frac{\partial FR}{\partial d} > 0. \tag{4.7}$$

Furthermore, unborrowed reserves at commercial banks are defined as

$$UR = HP - MC \tag{4.8}$$

where HP is a high powered money and MC is currency in the hands of the public. The central bank determines the amount of high powered money through the buying and selling of government securities. The public, however, determines the amount of those reserves that are held in the form of currency outside banks. Therefore, the amount of unborrowed reserves held in commercial banks is determined as the residual to the public's demand for currency. Thus

$$UR = HP - MC(y) \tag{4.9}$$

where it is assumed that the public's demand for currency is a function of income.

Substituting (4.9) and (4.7) into (4.6) it is shown that supply is endogenously determined according to the expression

$$MD_S = \frac{HP-MC(y)-FR(i,d)}{z_D} . \qquad (4.10)$$

Thus, the central bank controls the total amount of high powered money, the public determines its demands for currency,and the banks determine their holdings of excess reserves in accordance with available market interest rates.[4] When the level of interest rates is high, the opportunity cost of holding excess reserves is high and banks economize by lowering these reserves. When interest rates are low, the opposite effect occurs. Consequently, the amount of liabilities supplied by banks is a positive function of interest rates.

In this study this contemporary theory of money supply is applied to the historical case of the United States in the pre-Civil War period. Because the institutional framework of the monetary system at that time differs from that of the modern period, some modifications are required. Nevertheless, much of the basic analysis remains the same. The objective of this approach is to derive an empirically testable specification describing the willingness of the commercial banking system to supply liabilities during the early 1800's. Once again it is assumed that the total amount of high powered money is exogenous to the monetary system. In the context of the pre-Civil War period, high powered money consists of total specie, that is specie held by the public plus specie held by the banks. This sum is assumed to be determined entirely outside the monetary system by such variables as mining discoveries, technical progress, and events abroad. It should be noted that this sum was not under the regulatory authority of the Second Bank while it existed. The supply of currency in the hands of the public is assumed to be demand determined, as in the contemporary context.

Based upon these assumptions, the supply of bank liabilities is endogenously determined through bank portfolio behavior. In both the current and pre-Civil War period, bank portfolios were composed of assets from the general categories of government and municipal securities, commercial loans, and mortgages.[5] Portfolio theory suggests that commercial banks adjust the composition of their asset holdings in accordance with the pattern of relevant interest rates. Thus a rise in the yield on government securities induces banks to hold more of such securities. As a result, banks draw down on their level of excess reserves which increases the money supply.

In the historical framework, the basic model of the supply of bank liabilities is derived as follows. Total reserves, TR, which are actually total specie, are divided into specie held by the public (currency), MC, and bank specie, BS so that

$$TR = MC + BS \tag{4.11}$$

Since total reserves are exogenous and currency is determined by the public, the quantity of bank specie is exogenous to the banking sector.[6] In the modern case, this figure is divided into required reserves and excess reserves minus borrowings. Since legal reserve requirements did not exist prior to the founding of the Federal Reserve System, no such figures can actually be calculated for the pre-Civil War period. Nevertheless, it can be assumed that part of bank specie must have been held as the equivalent of required reserves, that is, that quantity of reserves which banks believed were needed at a minimum to keep the bank operating smoothly and support the level of deposits. Thus, bank specie is defined as

$$BS = MR + ER \tag{4.12}$$

where MR is minimum reserves and ER excess reserves.

Borrowed reserves are not included in this model for two reasons. First, although the question of whether the Second National Bank was a central bank is difficult to settle,[7] it is clear that the Second National Bank was not a "lender of last resort," since it never established a formal discount rate mechanism as exists today. A second reason for excluding borrowing is that although there was some interbank borrowing during the early 1800's, this did not increase the overall quantity of reserves available to the banking system. Thus, the discount rate has no role in this analysis.

Therefore, bank specie or total reserves is considered to be equal to minimum reserves, defined as either a constant or exogenously determined fraction, z_D, of bank liabilities needed to be held as reserves, plus excess specie reserves, so that

$$BS = z_D MD + ER \tag{4.13}$$

which can be rewritten as

$$MD_s = \frac{1}{z_D} (BS - ER) \tag{4.14}$$

In this formulation, excess specie is similar to the contemporary concept of free reserves. That is, banks were free to determine the quantity of such reserves. Consequently, excess specie is a negative function of the yields on assets that the banks regard as close substitutes for reserves since these asset yields represent the opportunity cost of holding reserves. Therefore,

$$ER = ER(i) \quad \frac{\partial ER}{\partial i} < 0, \tag{4.15}$$

where i represents the appropriate interest rate, which presumably is the government bond yield although other rates might also be relevant. Thus making the appropriate substitution and rewriting (4.14) yields

$$MD_s = \frac{1}{z_D} \; (BS - ER\,(i)) \quad \frac{\partial ER}{\partial i} < 0 \tag{4.16}$$

which is the basic supply model, termed Model I, tested in this study. Thus, the supply of bank liabilities can be broken into a function of the quantity of bank specie, which is observable, and excess reserves, which are a function of interest rates, also observable. Furthermore, the supply of bank liabilities is positively related to the level of bank specie and also to the level of interest rates since higher interest rates induce lower excess reserves and hence a higher supply of bank liabilities.

An alternative specification for the money supply, termed Model II, which is applicable to the pre-Civil War period is based on an approach initially developed by Ronald Teigen.[8] The formulation is derived from the expression (4.16):

$$MD = \frac{1}{z_D} \quad (BS-ER(i))$$

Since it is assumed that bank specie is exogenous to the commercial banking system, a new variable, MD*, can be defined as

$$MD^{*} = \frac{1}{z_D}(BS) \qquad (4.17)$$

This variable is interpreted as the maximum quantity of bank liabilities which can be supported by the given quantity of bank specie. This indicates what quantity of bank liabilities the banks could be induced to supply if interest rates are sufficiently high so that holdings of excess reserves are reduced to zero.

Dividing both sides of expression (4.16) by MD* yields

$$\frac{MD}{MD^*} = 1 - \frac{ER(i)}{z_D MD^*} \quad \frac{\partial ER}{\partial i} < 0 \tag{4.18}$$

Therefore, the ratio of bank liabilities to the maximum supply of bank liabilities is essentially a positive function of interest rates. The higher the rate of interest, the lower excess reserves and the higher the stock of bank liabilities that banks desire to supply.

Thus, two money supply specifications have been derived which can be empirically tested within the framework of pre-Civil War monetary conditions. In each case it is assumed that reserves are divided into two distinct but unobservable segments, one part the minimum reserves needed to maintain operations which are not interest elastic and the other part excess reserves which are interest elastic. Consequently, for empirical purposes, the supply of bank liabilities can be specified in linear form as

$$MD_s = b_o + b_1 BS + b_2 i \tag{4.19}$$

where both bank specie and interest rates are observable. Both coefficients b_1 and b_2 should be positive and b_1 can be considered an estimate of $1/z_D$ where z_D is the reserve ratio. Thus b_1 indicates what quantity of bank liabilities is supplied by an additional dollar of bank specie, ceteris paribus. This specification is useful because it affords an estimate of the marginal money supply multiplier. The other empirical specification is derived from (4.18):

$$\frac{MD}{MD^*} = b_0 + b_1 i \qquad (4.20)$$

where b_1 is assumed positive and where MD/MD* is a measure of money supply expansion. In the context of modern institutional arrangements, MD* is calculated as

$$MD^* = \frac{UR}{z_D} \qquad (4.21)$$

where UR is unborrowed reserves and z_D is the legal reserve requirement. For the pre-Civil War period MD* is derived in an alternative manner. First, the maximum value for MD/BS, the ratio of bank liabilities to bank specie, is obtained from the sample period data. It is implicitly assumed that when MD/BS is a maximum, excess reserves are zero. Then MD* is calculated as

$$MD^* = BS \left(\frac{MD}{BS}\right)_{Max} . \qquad (4.22)$$

Thus MD/MD* can be interpreted as an index of monetary expansion rather than an absolute measure. Because of both the stronger assumptions required to derive this model and the fact that it provides no explicit empirical estimate of the money multiplier, empirical testing with this specification is regarded primarily as a means of confirming results obtained with the first version, Model I, of the money supply equation (4.19).

4.2 Empirical Evidence

The two money supply models developed in section 4.1 are tested empirically over the same sample period, 1823 through 1859, that was used in testing the money demand models. The results are reported in Tables 4.1 and 4.2. The regressions are estimated using ordinary least squares but when the presence of serial correlation is indicated, the regressions are reestimated using the Cochrane-Orcutt (10) first order auto-regressive technique. The t statistics appear in parentheses below the coefficients. The specifications used for these regressions follow directly from the theoretical models. Bank liabilities defined as demand deposits plus notes in circulation is the same series used in the money demand section. Three interest rates are tested to determine which bank asset was a close substitute for bank reserves; RL, the long term government securities rate; RMUN, the municipal bond rate; and RCP, the commercial paper rate.

Table 4.1 reports the results for Model I, in

Table 4.2

Supply of Bank Liabilities;

Dependent Variable is Level of Bank Liabilities,

1823 - 1859

	BS	BS_{-1}	BS_{-2}	Σ BS	RL	RMUN
1)	1.4558 (2.25)			1.4558	-35.8430 (-2.08)	
2)	1.8745 (2.93)			1.8745		-59.2480 (-1.33)
3)	1.8600 (2.83)			1.8600		
4)	2.4046 (4.51)	2.0094 (4.00)		4.4140	-30.4869 (-1.93)	
5)	2.5033 (4.46)	1.8632 (3.42)		4.3665		-14.0531 (-.33)
6)	2.3812 (4.20)	1.7671 (3.20)		4.1423		
7)	2.5140 (4.58)	1.9089 (3.60)		4.4229		
8)	2.4083 (4.36)	1.6901 (3.04)	.9302 (1.27)	5.0286		
9)	2.4505 (4.64)	1.9456 (3.86)		4.3961		

Table 4.1

(continued)

	RCP	DUM	ΔCapital	Constant	R^2/SE	DW/Rho
1)				476.5070 (2.90)	.90 32.91	2.28 .96
2)				523.0031 (2.16)	.90 34.03	2.20 .94
3)	-1.8407 (-1.12)	44.5753 (1.19)		182.1136 (1.84)	.89 34.33	2.10 .93
4)				174.7890 (2.11)	.92 29.87	2.05 .66
5)				106.1803 (.49)	.91 31.33	2.08 .75
6)	-1.2485 (-.78)	36.6453 (1.08)		24.7459 (.55)	.91 31.22	2.06 .76
7)				33.9428 (.94)	.92 30.91	2.08 .73
8)				10.6677 (.28)	.92 30.64	2.13 .71
9)			.3725 (1.92)	30.6030 (.97)	.92 29.78	2.04 .70

which the dependent variable, the level of bank liabilities, is a function of the level of bank specie and interest rates, equation (4.19). In the first three equations, bank liabilities are a function of the current level of bank specie with each of the three asset rates entered individually. The coefficients of bank specie in these equations range between 1.5 and 1.9. This implies that if bank specie increases by one unit, the money supply is expanded by a factor of about one and a half or two. Given that the behavior of commercial banks during this period was effectively unrestricted, the size of this specie multiplier is unrealistically small. The results for the assets rates are disappointing. In equation (1) the coefficient of the bond rate, RL, is large and significant but has the wrong sign. In equations (2) and (3) both the municipal bond rate, RMUN, and the commercial paper rate, RCP, have incorrect negative signs although the low t statistics indicate that they are not statistically different from zero.

These preliminary interest rate results imply that the money supply during the early 1800's was not interest sensitive. It seems unlikely that the money supply could have been interest elastic and yet not be sensitive to one of the rates tested in this study. Moreover, the results for the bank specie variable imply that banks had an unrealistically strong desire for reserves relative to their liabilities. However the combination of these results and the high degree of serial correlation present in the residuals suggests the presence of specification error and the need for further refinement in the choice of independent variables.

Consequently, it was decided to investigate the low coefficients for bank specie by allowing for the possibility that banks did not adjust their asset portfolios immediately to changes in bank specie. Thus a bank specie variable with a one year lag is added to the specifications for equations (1) - (3). The results are reported as equations (4) - (6). Although the interest rate coefficients still have the incorrect sign, the results for bank specie are more reasonable than those previously obtained. The coefficients on the lagged value of bank specie are large and strongly significant and the coefficients on current bank specie increase. This provides strong evidence that banks did not fully adjust their asset portfolios within one year to changes in specie. Moreover, there is a sharp decline in autocorrelation of the residuals. The sums of the bank specie coefficients, which are reported in the fourth column of Table 4.1, indicate an overall specie multiplier greater than 4. These results imply that if bank specie increased by one unit, the money supply expanded through bank portfolio behavior, by more than four units. This is a more reasonable result and is similar to standard bank behavior in the modern context. Thus these findings provide no evidence of any irresponsible wildcat banking behavior which is often cited as characteristic of the pre-Civil War period.

Since all attempts to obtain positive interest rate coefficients failed, these variables are dropped from the final specification, equation (7). The money supply is reestimated as a function of bank specie only which implies no interest rate sensitivity. The specie multiplier in this equation is about 4.4.

Although the results with this specification are adequate, two further refinements are tested. First, since the results for lagging bank specie are strong, another lag on specie is included which appears as equation (8). The coefficient indicates that the effect of bank specie lagged two years is weak and fails to be significant. Thus the results for equation (7) are retained as the best description of money supply behavior. A final specification, equation (9), is estimated which includes a variable for the change in the capital stock of the banking system. The reason for including this variable is that during the early 1800's, particularly before 1840, some states restricted bank note issue or deposits to be a proportion of bank capital stock. Therefore, it is possible that an increase in the stock of bank capital in a given year increases the money stock. The variable has a small coefficient which has the correction positive sign and indicates that a one dollar increase in capital stock increases the money supply by about 40 cents. However, the capital stock coefficient is not significantly different from zero at the 5 percent level of significance and hence is not considered to be part of the final specification.

The empirical results for Model II in which the dependent variable is specified as MD/MD*, are reported in Table 4.2. For estimation purposes MD/MD* is related

Table 4.2

Supply of Bank Liabilities;Dependent Variable is MD/MD*, 1823-1859

	ΔBS	$ΔBS_{-1}$	RL	RMUN	RCP	DUM	ΔCapital	Constant	R^2/SE	DW/Rho
1)	-.0057 (-4.12)		-.1231 (-2.69)					1.2925 (6.01)	.56 .091	1.94 .55
2)	-.0053 (-3.78)			.0200 (.15)				.6227 (.95)	.48 .099	2.05 .67
3)	-.0052 (-4.16)				-.0058 (-1.23)	.2453 (2.41)		.4563 (4.62)	.54 .094	2.04 .81
4)	-.0053 (-3.85)							.7216 (14.48)	.50 .098	2.04 .68
5)	-.0059 (-3.58)	-.0013 (-.68)						.7273 (14.08)	.49 .098	2.12 .68
6)	-.0054 (-3.89)						.0010 (1.59)	.7113 (17.00)	.52 .096	1.95 .62

to interest rates in a linear regression of the form

$$\frac{MD}{MD^*} = b_o + b_1(i) \qquad (4.23)$$

where it is assumed that b_1 is positive. The i is again approximated by the three asset rates used in the first model.

In addition to these interest rates specified in equation (4.23), a variable is entered in the regressions in order to capture lags in money supply behavior. This variable is the change in bank specie which is explicitly included to account for the possible time lag required for commercial banks to issue loans or buy securities in response to sudden inflows of bank specie. Consequently, a sudden increase in bank specie in the short run, lowers MD/MD*. Hence MD/MD* is expected to be negatively related to recent changes in bank specie. It should be noted that this variable has no steady state impact on the money supply and that the level of bank specie is still implicitly part of the model.

In equations (1) - (3) ofTable 4.2, MD/MD* is estimated as a function of asset rates and the change in bank specie. As in the results for the first model, no interest rate sensitivity is discernible since both the bond rate, RL, and the commercial paper rate, RCP, have incorrect negative signs and the municipal bond rate, RMUN, has the correct positive sign but is not significantly different from zero. In each equation, however, the change in bank specie obtains a strongly significant negative sign. This indicates that banks only gradually adjusted their portfolios to sudden inflows of specie and that, as a result in the short run, MD/MD* was lowered. It should be noted that the fit of these equations is quite good considering the ratio construction of the dependent variable.[9]

In Model II the supply of money is not interest elastic, a result which confirms the finding obtained for the first model. Therefore, the interest rates are again dropped from the specification and MD/MD* is estimated as a simple function of the change in bank specie and a constant, equation (4). The R^2 is still fairly good, .50, and ΔBS obtains a strongly negative coefficient. In order to obtain more information about the length of time required by banks to adjust their portfolios after a sudden change in bank specie, another lag on bank specie was added in equation (5). Although ΔBS is still strongly negative, ΔBS_{-1} fails to obtain a coefficient significantly different from zero. Consequently, this variable is omitted from the specification.

The final variable tested is the change in capital stock, equation (6). As in Model I, the coefficient on capital stock is small and is not significant at the normal level of statistical confidence. Thus this variable is also dropped from the final specification.

Overall, two important conclusions are obtained from the empirical results for the money supply equation. First, money supply models are capable of explaining most of the variation found in the behavior of the money supply in the pre-Civil War period.[10] The equations for the level of the supply of bank liabilities, for example, have R^2's of over .90 and obtain sensible estimates of the bank specie multiplier. Second, there is no evidence for the key contemporary view that the quantity of bank liabilities supplied by the commercial banking sector is positively interest elastic. This implies that either the supply of money during the early 1800's must be viewed as an exogenous variable or that there may be specification error in the estimated equations, possibly due to a lack of structural stability over the sample period. Since both the demand and the supply of money for the pre-Civil War period have now been explored and tested, this question of structural stability becomes a central concern.

Chapter 5

THE BANK WAR AND THE STABILITY OF THE DEMAND AND SUPPLY FOR MONEY

5.1 Preliminary Evidence

Both demand and supply functions for money have been estimated based upon specifications derived from contemporary monetary theory and the results clearly demonstrate that standard monetary theory and econometric techniques are capable of explaining a body of data generated by an economic environment different from that of the contemporary United States. In general, both the demand functions for bank liabilities and currency during the pre-Civil War period produce results that are compatible with those produced by modern researchers to explain similar contemporary American phenomena. The supply of money results are also reasonable, although the implication that the supply of money does not endogenously respond to movements in interest rates differs from recent findings about the contemporary monetary system.

There remains, however, the second basic question to which this study is directed, specifically, whether the Bank War of the 1830's and the failure to recharter the Second National Bank had any repercussions on the economy. From a neo-Keynesian viewpoint, it is clear that if the Bank War had any effect on the economy, then there must have been an observable impact on the money market. Such an impact should be observable in the behavior of the money demand and supply functions. If these functions are stable then, from the viewpoint of modern economic analysis, the traditional view of the Bank War cannot be justified. That is, the economic disruptions of the 1830's cannot be attributed to the Bank War. Alternatively, if the functions are not stable, although the traditional view cannot be clearly confirmed, it can be concluded that the empirical evidence is not consistent with the new view of the Bank War that Jackson's financial policies did not affect the economy.[1]

Consequently in order to test for monetary stability, the basic supply and demand equations for money are estimated separately, first over the sample period of 1823-1835, and then over the period 1836-1859. The reason for splitting the equations in 1835-1836 is that 1835 was the last year that the Second National Bank operated as a national bank and that 1836 was the first year that the Bank operated as a state bank. A priori, if the stability of the functions is clear at this juncture then it is reasonable to assume that the functions are stable throughout the Bank War period. The specifications that are tested are those which had the best full sample empirical results based on the initial theoretical models. The results for the split demand for bank liabilities and currency equations and the split money supply regressions are found in Tables 5.1 and 5.2 respectively. In each case the results are striking.

It should be noted that the full sample estimation results for both the demand for bank liabilities and currency did not suggest any serious misspecification due to structural instability since the income and interest rate variables had large coefficients with the correct sign and were strongly significant. The estimation results for the separate periods, however, indicate that the behavior of the public with respect to the demand for money in the period of 1823-1835, equation (1a), differed

Table 5.1

Split Demand Equations

	ln Y	ln RL	Constant	R^2/SE	DW/Rho
1a) ln MD	1.7233	.9617	-4.7029	.79	1.39
1823-35	(6.93)	(.57)	(-1.67)	.158	
b) ln MD	.9790	-1.2478	1.9994	.92	2.25
1836-59	(4.84)	(-3.35)	(1.36)	.117	.65
c) ln MD	1.7211		-3.2564	.81	1.41
1823-35	(7.15)		(-2.89)	.153	
2a) ln MC	1.1172	3.2189	-7.4211	.56	1.86
1823-35	(3.88)	(1.63)	(2.28)	.183	
b) ln MC	1.7010	-.6606	-3.5837	.97	1.85
1836-59	(12.65)	(-1.85)	(-3.18)	.124	.39
c) ln MC	1.1098		-2.5797	.50	1.81
1823-35	(3.59)		(-1.79)	.196	

substantially from that of the period 1836-1859, equation (1b). The pattern of the income coefficients is quite interesting. The estimate of the income elasticity in the full sample period regression, (1) in Table 3.1, is approximately unity. From Table 5.1, however, the income elasticity of bank liabilities is much higher, 1.72, during the early period, but drops sharply to .98 after the National Bank lost its charter. Consequently, it is clear that the desirability of holding demand deposits and notes, given the level of interest rates, declined substantially after 1835. The interest rate elasticities in equations (1a) and (1b) also display a distinctive pattern. For the first half of the sample period, there is no discernible interest elasticity. The government bond rate variable has the wrong sign and is not significantly different from zero.[2] For the second part of the sample period, however, the government bond rate variable is negative and strongly significant. The size of the coefficient is almost identical to the full sample period coefficient reported in Table 3.1 equation (1). This indicates that the public's demand for bank liabilities became sensitive to the opportunity cost of holding money only after the Second National

Bank ceased operations under its federal charter.

The split sample estimation results for the demand for currency also show a sharp shift in structure. For the first half of the estimation period, equation (2a), the estimate of the income elasticity is 1.12 which is considerably smaller than the full sample result. The government bond rate variable has the wrong sign which indicates the lack of interest sensitivity of currency demand during the period of the Bank's federal charter. The estimation results for the period 1836-1859, equation (2b), are considerably different, however, from the earlier period. The income elasticity of currency demand is 1.70 and is strongly significant. Furthermore, the interest rate variable has a coefficient of -.66 and is significant at the 90 percent confidence level. This is the first indication that the demand for currency was interest elastic in the pre- Civil War period. Thus, as in the case of bank liabilities, the demand for currency was interest elastic only in the period after 1835. In contrast to the bank liabilities results, however, the income elasticity of currency rose substantially after the Bank lost its federal charter. That is, after 1835 the public's desire to hold currency heightened considerably.

Overall, the results obtained by reestimating the bank liabilitie and currency demand equations over the two distinct sample periods, 1823-1835 and 1836-1859, provide strong evidence that structural shifts occurred in both functions. The results suggest that with the end of the Second Bank the public's pattern of liquidity preference shifted from bank liabilities to specie. In addition, after 1835 the public's demand for money became interest elastic which indicates that sensitivity to the opportunity cost of holding money was initiated by the Bank War. Thus the estimation results provide substantial evidence that the demand for money was not structurally stable over the pre-Civil War period. Consequently the evidence contradicts the main hypothesis of the new view that Jackson's failure to recharter the Second Bank had no effect on the financial system. In general, the evidence indicates that the Bank War resulted in a sharp decline in the public's willingness to hold bank liabilities and induced a sharp rise in the demand for specie.

A similar estimation procedure is applied to the money supply equations developed previously.[3]

As in the case of money demand, the basic supply equations are reestimated separately, first over the period 1823-1835, and then over the period 1836-1859. The estimation results for the supply model in which the level of liabilities is a function of bank specie and the interest rate are reported in Table 5.2 as equations (1a) and (1b). The remaining equations apply to the model which specifies an index of money supply expansion as a function of the change in bank specie and the level of interest rates.

Again, the results are striking. Particularly important is the pattern of the interest rate coefficients. In the full period estimation, equation (4) in Table 4.1, no interest rate sensitivity for the supply of money is observed. In fact, the interest rate coefficients sometimes obtained a negative sign. These results imply that the commercial banks did not consider any of their specie to be excess holdings of reserves to be used for investment purposes. Consequently, a rise in interest rates could not induce a decline in these reserves and no expansion in the supply of liabilities could result without an increase in specie. In the early half of the sample period, equations (1a) and (2a) the interest rate variables

Table 5.2

Split Supply Equations

	BS	BS_{-1}	ΣBS	ΔBS	RL	Constant	R^2/SE	DW/Rho
1a) MD 1823-35	2.1531 (4.09)	4.5552 (7.90)	6.7083		78.8679 (2.94)	-369.8593 (-2.97)	.96 9.65	1.42 .36
b) MD 1836-59	2.3596 (3.19)	1.7829 (2.55)	4.1425		-36.6218 (-1.74)	221.0136 (1.74)	.88 35.98	2.00 .67
c) MD 1836-59	2.6600 (3.60)	1.7705 (2.39)	4.4305			29.2079 (.47)	.87 37.48	2.03 .74
2a) MD/MD* 1823-35				-.0155 (-5.13)	.2916 (1.84)	-.4677 (-.68)	.62 .071	2.05 .61
b) MD/MD* 1836-59				-.0046 (-3.43)	-.1166 (-2.39)	1.2466 (5.22)	.66 .088	1.82 .66
c) MD/MD* 1836-59				-.0041 (-2.96)		.6804 (8.92)	.59 .096	1.98 .74

have large coefficients with the correct positive sign. The coefficient in equation (1a) is significant at the 5 percent confidence level and in the index model, equation (2a), it is significant at the 10 percent level. In contrast, the rate variables for the later period are negative in both models. These results imply that after the expiration of the Bank's federal charter, commercial banks did not hold excess reserves available for investment and consequently, the interest elasticity of the supply of money dissipated. This suggests that the Bank War induced the commercial banks to become more conservative in their portfolio behavior.

The behavior of the bank specie variables in the split supply equations, (1a) and (1b), also shifts between the early and late periods. Although the specie variables are positive and significant in both periods, the size of the coefficients exhibit an interesting pattern, particularly in the size of the lagged specie variable. The sum of the specie coefficients in the early period, equation (1a), is over 50 percent larger than the sum for the later period, equation (1b). This means that during the early period as a result of a one unit increase in specie, the banking system expanded liabilities by almost seven units. Thus the specie multiplier was approximately 7, a figure almost twice as large as that estimated in the full period regression (7) in Table 4.1. Furthermore, this implies that during the later period for a given inflow of specie, banks kept a larger amount of that specie as reserves. These preliminary results indicate that there is no evidence that the post Bank period was characterized by the presence of so called wildcat banking,[4] that is, practices of excessive note issue with little or no reserve backing. If such practices were prevalent, then the sum of the specie coefficients should be larger in the later period than in the early period. In fact, the opposite results are observed in equations (1a) and (1b). This evidence is substantiated by the results obtained in equations (2a) and (2b). The early period coefficient for the change in the bank specie variable in equation (2a) is two and a half times as large as the coefficient in the later period, equation (2b). Since this variable captures the effect on bank portfolios of a sudden inflow of specie, the decrease in the size of this coefficient indicates that inflows of specie had relatively little effect on bank portfolios after 1835 and that consequently, a large proportion of specie inflows were retained by the banks. This implies that in the post Bank period, commercial banks desired a relatively high degree of specie reserves which is consistent with the results in equations (1a) and (1b).

Overall, the evidence of splitting these equations indicates that the behavior of the supply of money was not structurally stable over the pre-Civil War period. Thus the results refute the basic contention of the new view that Jackson's veto of the Second National Bank charter and subsequent financial policies did not affect the structural behavior of the banking system. While the evidence supports the traditional view that the Bank War had economic repercussions, it refutes the traditional contention of historians that the destruction of the National Bank ushered in a period of irresponsible banking behavior. In fact, the opposite result occurred. The commercial banking system in the aggregate sought to increase its ratio of specie to liabilities. Evidently, the commercial banks' desire for safety was so strong that their holdings of specie became insensitive to the opportunity cost of holding reserves. As a result, the supply of bank liabilities ceased to be responsive to interest rate increases and thus, supply became exogenously fixed by the level of bank specie.

These effects of the Bank War on the determinants of supply occurred simultaneously with the structural shift in the behavior of money demand. The empirical results indicate that the expiration of the Bank's federal charter induced a shift in the public's pattern of liquidity preference from bank liabilities to specie. Moreover, the public's sensitivity to the opportunity cost of holding money increased substantially. Thus, at the same time that the public's demand for money became very interest elastic, bank behavior became noticeably interest inelastic. In the next section contemporary monetary theory is used to investigate whether these changing patterns of interest rate substitution are consistent.

5.2 The Effects of a Shift in Demand on the Behavior of a Financial Intermediary

In the previous section, empirical evidence was presented that the failure to recharter the Second Bank was associated with a sharp increase in the interest elasticity of the demand for bank liabilities. Concomitantly, a shift occurred in commercial bank behavior which sharply diminished the interest elasticity of the supply of liabilities because the reserve holdings of commercial banks became less sensitive to the opportunity cost of holding specie. The reason for this change is probably the shift in the public's liquidity preference from bank liabilities to currency, as indicated by the pattern of the estimated income elasticities presented earlier in equations (1) and (2) in Table 5.1. It is reasonable to assume that the banking community was aware of this change in demand behavior and that the banks' desire for liquidity increased and their willingness to invest excess reserves lessened even with increases in the rate of interest available on competing assets such as government bonds.

In this section an alternative approach is explored in order to provide an explanation for the decline in the interest elasticity of the supply of bank liabilities. A theoretical model is developed to provide evidence that a decline in the interest elasticity of the supply of deposits can result directly from an increase in the interest elasticity of the public's demand for bank liabilities, such as occurred in the 1830's, even if no shift occurred in the banking sector's desire for liquidity. The model is derived from the theory of deposit rate setting at financial institutions which has been developed by Weber (66), Meyer (41), Goldfeld and Jaffee (25), and Slovin (50). The model is framed in microeconomic terms and analyzes the behavior of a financial intermediary which takes the public's demand for bank liabilities as given and seeks to maximize profit over a single period horizon. Furthermore the financial institution takes interest rates on securities as given and then determines the optimal yield on its liabilities by maximizing profits. Although regulatory constraints have prevented commercial banks from offering interest on demand deposits since the 1930's[5], there was no restriction in the pre-Civil War period and banks did offer positive yields on their deposits.[6]

The demand for deposits, MD, is assumed to be a positive function of the deposit rate, r, and income, Y, but a negative function of the open market interest rate, i. It is also assumed that there are diminishing returns to increases in the deposit rate. Thus, the public's demand for deposits can be written as

$$MD = MD(i, r, Y) \quad \frac{\partial MD}{\partial i} < 0; \frac{\partial MD}{\partial Y}, \frac{\partial MD}{\partial r} > 0; \frac{\partial^2 MD}{\partial r^2} < 0 \qquad (5.1)$$

There is no endogenous determination of reserve holdings and instead, the bank is assumed to hold a constant proportion, k, of its portfolio in interest bearing assets with (1 - k) held as reserves. Thus the profit function can be written as:

$$\pi = ikMD - rMD, \qquad (5.2)$$

where π is profit. The first order condition for a profit maximum is that

$$\frac{\partial \pi}{\partial r} = (ik - r)\frac{\partial MD}{\partial r} - MD = 0 \quad . \qquad (5.3)$$

This equation implicitly determines the profit maximizing deposit rate as a function of the open market interest rate, the liquidity ratio , and the parameters of the demand function. The second order condition for a profit maximum is that

$$(ik - r)\frac{\partial^2 MD}{\partial r^2} - 2\frac{\partial MD}{\partial r} < 0 \quad , \tag{5.4}$$

which holds in the neighborhood of equilibrium.

The comparative statics effect of a change in open market interest rates on deposits, dMD/di , is

$$\frac{dMD}{di} = \frac{\partial MD}{\partial r}\frac{dr}{di} + \frac{\partial MD}{\partial i} \quad . \tag{5.5}$$

The total derivative dr/di, the comparative statics effect of a change in open market rates on the deposit rate, is obtained by implicit differentiation of equation (5.3):

$$\frac{dr}{di} = \frac{-\left(\frac{k\partial MD}{\partial r}\frac{\partial MD}{\partial i}\right)}{(ik-r)\frac{\partial^2 MD}{\partial r^2} - 2\frac{\partial MD}{\partial r}} > 0 \quad . \tag{5.6}$$

This derivative is clearly positive from the signs of the partial derivatives in equation (5.1) and the second order condition. Thus, the effect of a change in open market rates on deposits is

$$\frac{dMD}{di} = \frac{-k\left(\frac{\partial MD}{\partial r}^2\right) + \frac{\partial MD}{\partial r}\frac{\partial MD}{\partial i}}{(ik - r)\frac{\partial^2 MD}{\partial r^2} - 2\frac{\partial MD}{\partial r}} + \frac{\partial MD}{\partial i} . \qquad (5.7)$$

The second term, the shift in the demand function, is negative, while the first term, the movement along the function, is positive so that the overall effect is ambiguous.

If the effect of a change in open market rates on demand, $\partial MD/\partial i$, is assumed to be a parameter in the model, the effect of a change in this elasticity on the quantity of deposits that the intermediary supplies, given a change in open market rates, dMD/di, can be solved for by differentiating (5.7). This yields

$$\frac{d\left(\frac{dMD}{di}\right)}{d\left(\frac{\partial MD}{\partial i}\right)} = \frac{+\frac{\partial MD}{\partial r}}{(ik - r)\frac{\partial^2 MD}{\partial r^2} - \frac{2\partial MD}{\partial r}} + 1 > 0 , \qquad (5.8)$$

which is clearly positive since the left hand term must be smaller than one half in absolute value.[7] Consequently, an increase in the interest elasticity of demand will result in a smaller impact of changes in open market rates on deposits. That is, the profit maximizing bank will supply less additional deposits for a given increase in open market rates.

This result suggests that even if the reserve holding pattern of commercial banks is not affected by a change in the structure of demand, then as a result of profit maximization behavior, fewer additional deposits will be supplied by the banking sector for a given increase in open market interest rates. This implies that the empirical results of the previous section, which indicate that the failure to recharter the Second National Bank increased the interest elasticity of the public's demand for bank liabilities but decreased the elasticity of supply, are consistent with the assumption of profit maximization behavior for the commercial bank sector.

5.3 The Pattern of Behavior of Money Demand and Supply over the Bank War Period

It has been shown that within the context of modern monetary analysis there is evidence to support the hypothesis that the failure to recharter the Second National Bank altered the behavior of the demand and supply of money. The Bank War, however, covered several years from Jackson's veto of the rechartering bill in 1832, to the expiration of the charter in 1836 and the bankruptcy of the Bank under a state charter in 1841. Consequently in order to provide more information about the exact pattern of the shifts in these functions, the demand and supply equations for money are reestimated in this section to allow for a split in the sample period for each year from 1832 to 1841.[8]

The estimation results for the demand for bank liabilities functions are reported in Table 5.3. The split regressions are estimated by ordinary least squares since failure of convergence often occurs when the Cochrane-Orcutt autoregressive technique is utilized. The government bond rate is reported only for the late half

TABLE 5.3

Stability Results for the Demand for Bank Liabilities

Sample Period	ln Y	ln RL	Constant	R^2/SE	DW
23 - 32	1.3864 (4.25)		-1.7333 (-1.16)	.65 .122	1.53
33 - 59	.6617 (6.92)	-1.6666 (-5.02)	4.4341 (5.14)	.82 .170	.71
23 - 33	1.3269 (5.62)		-1.4623 (-1.34)	.75 .116	1.45
34 - 59	.6406 (6.30)	-1.7090 (-5.00)	4.6193 (5.05)	.81 .172	.67
23 - 34	1.4735 (7.23)		-2.1302 (-2.25)	.82 .118	1.68
35 - 59	.6528 (5.92)	-1.6812 (-4.69)	4.5071 (4.53)	.81 .175	.59
23 - 35	1.7211 (7.15)		-3.2564 (-2.89)	.81 .153	1.41
36 - 59	.7497 (6.65)	-1.4445 (-4.09)	3.5941 (3.50)	.84 .163	.71
23 - 36	1.8563 (7.76)		-3.8713 (-3.45)	.82 .162	1.25
37 - 59	.9018 (9.14)	-1.1457 (-3.93)	2.2724 (2.55)	.91 [illegible]	.85

TABLE 5.3

(continued)

Sample Period	ln Y	ln RL	Constant	R^2/SE	DW
23 - 37	1.7271 (7.68)		-3.2791 (-3.09)	.81 .167	1.57
38 - 59	.9649 (9.33)	-1.0355 (-3.57)	1.7433 (1.89)	.91 .125	.97
23 - 38	1.6928 (8.32)		-3.1219 (-3.24)	.82 .162	1.56
39 - 59	1.1337 (11.48)	-.6666 (-2.55)	.2165 (.24)	.95 .102	1.40
23 - 39	1.5107 (7.21)		-2.2805 (-2.29)	.76 .182	1.27
40 - 59	1.2180 (11.38)	-.5035 (-1.88)	.5157 (-.54)	.95 .097	1.72
23 - 40	1.3623 (6.34)		-1.5957 (-1.55)	.70 .200	.94
41 - 59	1.3098 (10.56)	-.3346 (-1.16)	-1.2995 (-1.19)	.95 .095	1.90

of the sample periods since the variable has the wrong sign or is not significant for the first half of each estimation period and thus is omitted from the specification. The statistical fit of these equations is quite good with about 80 to 95 percent of the total variation explained by the independent variables. Since the reported R^2's have been adjusted for degrees of freedom, somewhat lower R^2's are obtained for the very early or very late samples because of the small number of observations. In general the government bond rate coefficients for the late period regressions are large and strongly significant. This indicates that the public's demand for money was interest elastic during most of the post Bank period and probably even as early as the years following Jackson's veto. The pattern of the income coefficients is especially interesting. In each sample period the impact of the income variable is large and signifcantly positive with some t statistics in excess of eleven. Nevertheless, the pattern of the income coefficients changes as the break in the sample period is altered. These results add considerable insight to the preliminary shift results reported in Table 5.1. Specifically, the income elasticities for the early sample periods are almost twice as large as those of the late periods with this differential gradually declining as the split in the sample period moves towards 1840. Thus the results indicate, that during and after the period of the Bank War the public's desire to hold bank liabilities given the level of income declined sharply. From 1832 until the end of the Second Bank's federal charter, a one percent increase in income increased the public's holdings of bank liabilities by about 1.5 percent. After that period however, a similar increase in income induced less than a one percent increase in liabilities. The pattern of the estimation results suggest that this change occurred gradually throughout the period 1832-1840.

Consequently, the empirical results are consistent in two ways with the hypothesis that the Bank War decreased the public's willingness to hold bank liabilities. One, apparently the events of the Bank War period sharply lowered the income elasticity of the demand for liabilities. Two, the public evidently began to regard government bonds as a substitute for bank liabilities so that holdings of bank liabilities became strongly interest elastic.

The results of the split equations for the demand for currency are reported in Table 5.4.[9] These results substantiate the previous findings for bank liabilities and indicate that a structural shift in the money market occurred over a period of several years during the 1830's. Again, the interest rate variable is statistically zero in the early period regressions and thus is omitted from the final specifications. From the late period results, it appears that the public demand for currency did not become measurably sensitive to interest rates until 1836, the year the Bank lost its charter. Prior to 1836, the rate coefficients in the late samples are quite small and not significantly different from zero. After 1835, the interest elasticity is approximately unity which is quite large and indicates the importance of the currency component of the demand for money for the period after the end of the Second National Bank's federal charter. Moreover the income elasticity of currency is substantially different between the pre and post periods but over time the pattern is opposite to that obtained for bank liabilities. More specifically,

TABLE 5.4

Stability Results for the Demand for Currency

Sample Period	ln Y	ln RL	Constant	R^2/SE	D.W.
23 - 32	.4875 (1.35)		.2517 (.15)	.08 .134	1.33
33 - 59	2.1770 (14.67)	.0802 (.16)	-7.4147 (-5.53)	.91 .263	.60
23 - 33	.8078 (2.80)		-1.2062 (-.90)	.41 .141	1.54
34 - 59	2.0749 (14.45)	-.1246 (-.26)	-6.5212 (-5.04)	.91 .243	.70
23 - 34	.7559 (3.24)		-.9697 (-.89)	.46 .135	1.66
35 - 59	1.8828 (18.84)	-.5608 -(1.73)	-4.7605 (-5.28)	.95 .159	1.05
23 - 35	1.1098 (3.59)		-2.5797 (-1.79)	.50 .196	1.81
36 - 59	1.7664 (18.84)	-.8450 (-2.88)	-3.6642 (-4.30)	.96 .136	1.27
23 - 36	1.4885 (3.71)		-4.3014 (-2.29)	.50 .271	1.14
37 - 59	1.7334 (16.59)	-.9098 (-2.95)	-3.3374 (-3.58)	.96 .137	1.30

TABLE 5.4

(continued)

Sample Period	ln Y	ln RL	Constant	R^2/SE	D.W.
23 - 37	1.8679 (4.41)		-6.0407 (-3.02)	.57 .315	.92
38 - 59	1.7295 (14.86)	-.9168 (-2.81)	-3.3441 (-3.22)	.96 .140	1.29
23 - 38	2.1095 (5.07)		-7.1489 (-3.63)	.62 .331	.85
39 - 59	1.6861 (12.14)	-1.0115 (-2.75)	-2.9518 (-2.37)	.95 .143	1.34
23 - 39	2.3149 (5.97)		-8.0977 (-4.40)	.68 .337	.84
40 - 59	1.6797 (10.35)	-1.0239 (-2.52)	-2.8963 (-2.01)	.95 .147	1.34
23 - 40	2.4371 (6.74)		-8.6616 (-5.02)	.72 .335	.83
41 - 59	1.6558 (8.34)	-1.0678 (-2.31)	-2.6924 (-1.54)	.94 .151	1.34

the income elasticity of currency demand during the late sample periods is more than twice as large as the elasticity obtained from the corresponding equations for the early sample periods. This indicates that for a given level of income, the public's demand for currency rose sharply during the 1830's, the years of the bank crises, while its demand for bank liabilities slackened considerably.

Overall, the empirical results on the stability of the demand side of the money market provide substantial evidence to support the hypothesis that the Bank War induced changes in the pattern of the public's demand for money. First, the overall pattern of the estimation results indicates that the functions are not structurally stable over the pre-Civil War period and that the period after the failure to recharter the Second National Bank must be analyzed separately from the earlier period. Second, the estimation results suggest that the structural shift cannot be confined to any one specific year, but developed gradually beginning with the 1832 veto of the Bank charter and continuing at least through the expiration of the federal charter in 1836. Third, the results indicate that the Bank War induced the public to be more sensitive to the rate of return on competing assets so that, ceteris paribus, the public became less desirous of holding a given quantity of money after the Bank's charter expired. Fourth, during the period of the Bank War the public's pattern of demand for currency versus bank liabilities distinctly shifted. Prior to the Bank War, at a given level of income, the public displayed a preference for bank liabilities compared to specie. With the advent of the Bank War, however, the public's desire for specie heightened while its demand for bank liabilities declined. This shift from bank liabilities to currency is a strong indication that the Bank War induced public concern and uncertainty about the future course of financial affairs.

Since preliminary results in Table 5.2 indicate a lack of structural stability for the money supply functions, these equations are also reestimated allowing for a split in the sample period for each year from 1832 to 1841. The regression results for the supply equation in which the level of bank liabilities is specified as the dependent variable are reported in Table 5.5. Since the government bond rate has the wrong sign for each late

TABLE 5.5

Stability Results for the Supply of Bank Liabilities; Dependent Variable is MD

Sample Period	BS	BS_{-1}	BS	RL	Constant	R^2/SE	DW/Rho
23 - 32	2.0377 (1.85)	8.7750 (8.35)	10.8127	82.9592 (4.49)	-472.6982 (-5.19)	.94 5.84	2.57 -.09
33 - 59	2.5233 (3.68)	1.9179 (2.80)	4.4412		32.8042 (.57)	.87 35.87	2.07 .74
23 - 33	2.8089 (3.38)	8.5094 (8.27)	11.3183	87.4283 (4.67)	-502.3185 (-5.51)	.95 5.85	2.11 -.06
34 - 59	2.5282 (3.61)	1.9282 (2.73)	4.4564		31.5037 (.52)	.86 36.63	2.07 .74
23 - 34	1.1318 (2.28)	9.3976 (7.94)	10.5294	92.7522 (4.03)	-508.9898 (-4.51)	.96 7.25	2.35 .06
35 - 59	2.5686 (3.53)	1.9092 (2.63)	4.4778		32.0068 (.52)	.86 37.38	1.99 .74
23 - 35	2.1530 (4.09)	4.5552 (7.90)	6.7082	78.8679 (2.94)	-369.8593 (-2.97)	.96 9.65	1.42 .36
36 - 59	2.6600 (3.60)	1.7705 (2.39)	4.4305		29.2079 (.47)	.87 37.48	2.03 .74
23 - 36	2.1351 (4.26)	4.4596 (8.86)	6.5944	74.5120 (3.26)	-348.3173 (-3.32)	.97 9.22	1.41 .37
37 - 59	2.7088 (3.58)	1.8221 (2.40)	4.5309		21.8253 (.34)	.87 38.30	1.91 .73

TABLE 5.5

(continued)

Sample Period	BS	BS_{-1}	BS	RL	Constant	R^2/SE	DW/Rho
23 - 37	2.4469 (2.59)	3.5413 (3.85)	5.9882	11.5056 (.29)	-61.5711 (-.34	.91 17.14	1.55 .17
38 - 59	2.4880 (3.25)	1.6216 (2.09)	4.1096		54.2022 (.73)	.87 37.93	2.13 .78
23 - 38	2.0524 (2.66)	3.6384 (4.39)	5.6902	27.6849 (.75)	-125.4485 (-.74)	.91 16.64	1.87 .33
39 - 59	2.5007 (3.17)	1.6118 (2.00)	4.1125		54.8898 (.71)	.87 38.95	2.10 .78
23 - 39	2.7311 (3.13)	2.1352 (2.82)	4.8663	-2.8253 (-.07)	24.9753 (.13)	.86 20.19	1.78 .48
40 - 59	2.2988 (2.74)	1.6690 (2.04)	3.9678		70.1864 (.87)	.87 39.41	2.22 .78
23 - 40	2.5752 (3.09)	2.1795 (2.97)	4.7547	-6.8337 (-.18)	44.6992 (.25)	.86 19.68	1.92 .54
41 - 59	2.2745 (2.62)	1.5753 (1.77)	3.8498		80.5359 (.91)	.86 40.48	2.23 .78

period regression, this variable is omitted from the reported equations. This implies that no measurable interest rate sensitivity is discernible in the behavior of the supply of money after the Bank War period. Nevertheless, the estimation results indicate that the supply of money was interest elastic during the early part of the period. The coefficients of the government bond rate for the sample 1823-1832 through 1823-1836 period are large with t statistics in excess of three. It should be noted that this interest rate sensitivity is present only until 1836, the year the Second National Bank obtained a state charter. When the years following 1836 are included in the sample period, the decline in the interest rate coefficients is substantial. Eventually, the coefficients are negative but are not statistically significant. Thus the pattern of interest rate coefficients suggests that the Bank War induced a shift in the commercial banking sector's willingness to supply liabilities. Prior to the termination of the Second Bank's charter, an increase in interest rates induced the commercial banks to lower their holdings of excess reserves and increase the supply of money. After the Bank War, the money supply became exogenous since bank reserve behavior became insensitive to movements in the interest rate. The pattern of the coefficients for the bank specie variables provides further insight into the change in commercial bank behavior. The sum of the bank specie coefficients for each equation for the sample periods 1823-1832 through 1823-1834 is about ten. This implies that the banks regarded their minimum reserve ratio to be approximately .1. Together with the high interest rate elasticities estimated for these same periods, these results imply that banks had substantial quantities of reserves which were interest sensitive. Thus, during the period of the Bank's operation as a federal bank, the commercial banking system maintained a relatively low ratio of necessary reserves to liabilities. In contrast, for the late sample periods the sum of the bank specie coefficients is about four. Since there is no discernible sensitivity of reserves to interest rates in these samples, the implication is that commercial banks regarded all reserves as necessary to support their level of liabilities and maintained a marginal reserve ratio of about .25. To some extent the shift in behavior between these regimes was gradual, but it is clear that there was a sharp increase in 1835 in what the bank's regarded as their minimum reserve ratio . This shift can be seen by comparing the sum of the bank specie coefficients which in the regression for 1823-1834 is 10.5 but only 6.7 in the equation for 1823- 1835. Since the interest rate variable is strongly significant for the period 1823-1836 yet statistically zero for the sample period 1823-1837, it is clear that the interest sensitivity of reserves ended in 1836.

In general, these results imply that after the termination of the Second National Bank's federal charter in 1836, the commercial banks recognized that the public was increasingly wary of holding bank liabilities and had a liquidity preference for specie. Consequently, the banking sector's estimate of the reserve ratio needed to maintain operations increased and eventually commercial banks came to regard all of their specie holdings as required reserves. Thus a rise in interest rates, after this time, could no longer induce a reduction in reserve holdings and an expansion in the supply of bank liabilities.

The regression results for the money supply model in which the ratio of MD/MD^* is specified as the dependent variable confirm the above findings, but are not as useful as the results for the previous model because the bank specie multiplier does not explicity appear as an independent variable. The empirical results, which are reported in Table 5.6, imply that excess reserves were interest elastic only for the period 1823-1836. For that sample period, the interest rate coefficient is .29 and has a t statistic of over two. Beginning in the period 1823-1837, the coefficient falls sharply to .15 and is statistically insignificant thereafter.

Overall, the conclusions of this analysis of the structural stability of the supply of money closely parallel those obtained for the demand for money and further evidence is provided to support the hypothesis that the government's failure to recharter the Second National Bank altered the pattern of money supply behavior. First, the estimation results indicate that money supply behavior was not stable over the pre-Civil War period and that the period should be analyzed as two separate samples divided by the Bank War. More specifically, the shifts in this function occurred between 1835-1837. Second, prior to 1837 commercial banks behaved in a manner which suggests that a portion of their specie was held as excess reserves, and that such holdings were sensitive to movements in interest

TABLE 5.6

Stability Results for the Supply of Bank Liabilities; Dependent Variable is MD/MD*

Sample Period	$BS-BS_{-1}$	RL	Constant	R^2/SE	DW/Rho
23 - 32	-.0284 (-3.62)	.4418 (2.11)	-1.1693 (-1.27)	.60 .072	1.35 .36
33 - 59	-.0049 (-3.58)		.6926 (10.49)	.56 .098	2.02 .72
23 - 33	-.0218 (-3.46)	.3788 (2.00)	-.8631 (1.04)	.57 .073	1.62 .52
34 - 59	-.0049 (-3.51)		.6934 (9.99)	.55 .100	2.00 .72
23 - 34	-.0160 (-3.90)	.2922 (1.76)	-.4625 (-.64)	.56 .074	1.99 .62
35 - 59	-.0047 (-3.29)		.7061 (9.27)	.56 .100	1.82 .74
23 - 35	-.0155 (5.13)	.2916 (1.84)	-.4677 (-.68)	.62 .070	2.05 .61
36 - 59	-.0041 (-2.96)		.6804 (8.92)	.59 .096	1.98 .74
23 - 36	-.0155 (-5.42)	.2905 (2.03)	-.4633 (-.74)	.67 .067	2.06 .61
37 - 59	-.0041 (-2.90)		.6722 (9.23)	.57 .097	1.78 .72

TABLE 5.6

(continued)

Sample Period	$BS-BS_{-1}$	RL	Constant	R^2/SE	DW/Rho
23 - 37	-.0142 (-3.72)	.1556 (.85)	.0866 (.11)	.43 .086	1.76 .51
38 - 59	-.0042 (-3.09)		.6923 (7.71)	.61 .095	2.02 .78
23 - 38	-.0132 (3.89)	.1071 (.64)	.3027 (.41)	.47 .083	2.23 .47
39 - 59	-.0041 (2.91)		.6997 (7.48)	.60 .097	2.02 .77
23 - 39	-.0087 (-2.76)	.0004 (.01)	.7414 (.91)	.27 .095	1.92 .47
40 - 59	-.0042 (-2.81)		.7064 (7.33)	.61 .099	2.04 .77
23 - 40	-.0091 (3.14)	-.0143 (-.08)	.8012 (1.06)	.33 .093	2.05 .52
41 - 59	-.0041 (2.61)		.7185 (7.41)	.60 .101	2.04 .76

rates. After 1836, however, the empirical results imply that banks considered all their specie essential to maintaining their operations. Thus reserve holdings became insensitive to interest rate movements, and the period of an endogenous money supply ended. Third, the banks apparently considered the reserve ratio needed to maintain their liabilities to be fairly low, about .10, in the period 1823-1834. Afterward however, the banking sector evidently desired higher reserve rates in order to respond to the public's steady shift in liquidity preference from bank liabilities to specie.

5.4 The Historical Implications

This study has analyzed the determinants of the demand and supply of money during the pre-Civil War period and has examined the pattern and character of the structural shifts which occurred during the period of the Bank War. On the basis of this evidence, the major financial events of the Bank War period can be put into new perspective. When the data are analyzed within the framework of formal theoretical models of money demand and supply, the empirical evidence is not consistent with either the traditional interpretation or the "revisionist" view.

The traditional historical view of the Bank War period is that Jackson's failure to recharter the Second National Bank removed any effective restraint from the commercial banking system. As a result, financial liabilities were issued in excess of an amount justified by the banks' holding of specie. In combination with Jackson's financial policies,[10] this speculation culminated in the Panic of 1837, which was characterized by a large number of bank failures, and led to an extended period of economic recession. The empirical evidence presented in this study, however, contradicts most of the hypotheses of the traditional view. The estimation results indicate that although the Bank War affected the banking system it did not initiate a period of speculative bank behavior. In fact, the opposite effect is observed, that is, the commercial banking system became very cautious in its policies of holding specie reserves relative to liabilities and did not create an excessive expansion of the money supply. Since banks became so conservative, the Panic of 1837 cannot be attributed to speculative banking practices.

The new view of the Bank War diverges considerably from the viewpoint traditionally held by historians. For example, Temin's analysis (56) indicates that no decline in the ratio of reserves to the total money supply was initiated by the termination of the Second National Bank's federal charter. Thus Temin concludes that Jackson's veto of the charter had no economic effects since bank behavior remained the same throughout the entire period. Furthermore, he indicates that the Panic of 1837 was precipitated by international financial events.

Since Jackson had no control over such international developments, he can not be held responsible for the economic consequences of the Panic of 1837. The results presented in this study demonstrate that the empirical evidence is inconsistent with Temin's conclusions. The findings indicate that the failure to recharter the Second National Bank affected the public's willingness to hold bank liabilities and the willingness of the commercial banking system to supply those liabilities. More specifically, throughout the period of the Bank War, the public's pattern of liquidity preference, gradually but consistently, shifted from bank liabilities to specie. It is likely that this shift in behavior was indicative of both the public's increased fears and uncertainty about financial affairs after the demise of the Second National Bank, and the commercial banking system's awareness of this change in the pattern of the public's behavior. As profit maximizing intermediaries, the commercial banks responded by increasing their desire for specie relative to liabilities. As a result of this increased desire for liquidity, the commercial banking system became interest inelastic in its reserve holding behavior. It is likely that this induced the sharp contraction in bank liabilities which resulted in the Panic of 1837. If international events initiated the Panic of 1837, any effects must have been transmitted through the specie flow mechanism since the United States was on the bimetalic standard.[11] However, throughout this period the level of domestic specie increased. Although there were exports of specie, mining production more than compensated for such outflows. Consequently it is unlikely that the Panic of 1837 was caused by international events.

The historical implications of this study are substantiated when the empirical results on the shift in the money demand and supply functions found in Tables 5.3 - 5.6, are examined. Jackson vetoed the bill for the rechartering of the Bank in 1832. The empirical results indicate that until this year the income elasticity of the demand for currency remained fairly low compared to that for bank liabilities. After the veto a gradual, but steady increase occurs in the public's demand for currency. For the sample 1823-1833 the estimate of the income elasticity rises to .81 and is .76 for the sample period 1823-1834. For the demand for liabilities, the income elasticity remains approximately 1.40. Thus, although the Bank's charter did not expire until 1836, the public apparently showed some concern by increasing its currency holdings. This rise in currency demand began several years prior to the Specie Circular of 1836. The equations for the supply of liabilities for this period, Table 5.5, indicate that the banks did not adjust their pattern of reserves at this point, probably because of the large increase in total specie which occurred in 1834 and could accommodate both the demands of the public and the banks for currency.

By the end of 1835, however, the results indicate that conditions rapidly changed. By this time it must have been clear that the Bank's charter would actually expire in March 1836. The estimate of the income elasticity of currency rises sharply to 1.11 and the specie held by banks fell. The results show the pattern of bank behavior changed to take account of the public's increased demands for specie. For the sample period 1823 - 1835 the estimate of the bank specie multiplier falls from about 11 to 6.7 which indicates a sharp rise in the reserve ratio which banks considered necessary to maintain the acceptance of their liabilities. This implies that banks must have contracted their asset and liability holdings. Nevertheless, the interest elasticity of the banks remained high. This indicates that the banking system still acted to reduce its holdings of excess reserves in response to a rise in interest rates and increased the supply of liabilities. The results for the sample period 1823-1836 follow the same pattern. The demand for currency, ceteris paribus, rose and the bank specie multiplier fell but the interest elasticity of the commercial banking sector remained high. Throughout this period the income elasticity of bank liabilities was stable, indicating that the public was willing to hold bank liabilities but desired larger holdings of currency.

By 1837, however, a change occurred. The demand for currency continued to rise sharply as indicated by an estimate of the income elasticity of 1.87 for the sample period 1823-1837. Much of this increased demand must have come from bank holdings of specie which fell in 1837 as in the previous two years. As a result, bank behavior apparently became cautious since the results indicate that holdings of reserves became interest inelastic. Thus bank liabilities had to contracted in order for the banks to attain their desired reserve ratios. On the demand side, the public was apparently willing to hold bank liabilities, ceteris paribus, as indicated by the sizeable income elasticity in the money demand equation for the sample period 1823-1837. Because of the substantial decrease in the supply elasticity, demand and supply must have been equated via a reduction in demand alone since a rise in interest rates could no longer induce an increase in the supply of liabilities. It was this contraction in liabilities that probably precipitated the Panic of 1837. That is, it is likely that the Panic of 1837 occurred because of a sharp increase in the public's demand for currency which induced a rise in the commercial banking sector's desired reserve ratio and eventually curbed its willingness to supply more liabilities even with increases in interest rates. By 1837 the Banks behaved as if they had no excess reserves, only reserves necessary to support liabilities. Consequently, since the money market must clear at each point in time, the quantity of liabilities had to fall. Effectively, both the public and the banks increased their demand for high powered money, that is, specie. Since the quantity of specie was fixed in the short run, a severe monetary contraction was inevitable. Had a central bank existed, this situation could have been counteracted by increasing the volume of high powered money, either by printing more currency or the equivalent of open market operations.[12] But the absence of a national currency and a central bank made such a solution impossible in 1837.

Chapter 6

CONCLUSIONS

Two basic conclusions are drawn from this study. First, contemporary monetary theory and econometric techniques are powerful tools for analyzing the financial structure of the United States during the early nineteenth century. Equations for the demand and supply of money were estimated for the period 1823-1859 which effectively explained the behavior of both the public and commercial banking sector. The results indicate that historical events can be explained by contemporary theoretical modeling and econometric techniques, instead of being treated as unique subjects, each requiring a different explanation.

The second basic conclusion of this study is that the Bank War of the 1830's affected the American economy because it altered the pattern of financial behavior. Both the money demand and supply functions were tested for stability. The results indicated that sharp shifts occurred in the structure of both relationships. Furthermore, there is evidence that this structural instability developed gradually over the period demarcated by Jackson's veto of the rechartering bill of 1832 and the expiration of the federal charter of the Second National Bank in 1836.

Prior to the Bank War, the evidence implies that the public displayed a preference for bank liabilities compared to specie and was not sensitive to the opportunity cost of holding money. On the supply side, the commercial banking sector maintained only small quantities of reserves to support their liabilities and was strongly interest elastic in their holdings of excess reserves.

During the period of the Bank War, the public's liquidity preference shifted from bank liabilities to specie and became interest elastic. At the same time, the banks became more conservative in their reserve behavior. Banks held a larger proportion of reserves to support their liabilities and became insensitive to the opportunity cost of holding specie. As a result, the money supply became interest inelastic and therefore fixed by the supply of bank specie. Thus, there is no evidence that wildcat banking practices resulted from the failure to recharter the Second National Bank. The shift in the liquidity preference of both the public and the banks increased the demand for specie. Since the supply of specie was exogenous in the short run and the supply of liabilities was interest inelastic, the quantity of bank liabilities had to fall and a severe monetary contraction, the Panic of 1837, was inevitable.

APPENDIX A

In this appendix, the sources and characteristics of early 19th century financial data are discussed and evaluated. First, the general condition of the available data is reviewed and second, the definitions of the series for demand deposits and currency are explained.

With the establishment of the National Banking System in 1863, the federal government initiated the official collection of financial data on a regular and systematic basis.[1] Since both individual bank balance sheets and aggregated state data were published yearly in the _Annual Report of the Comptroller of the Currency_ (63) to Congress, research in the area of post Civil War monetary affairs has been able to draw upon an easily accessible, official source of financial data. Thus, data problems in such studies are primarily confined to questions of the most relevant definition and the proper level of aggregation for the appropriate financial variables.[2]

The official collection of financial data prior to the establishment of the National Banking System was more limited in scope and less detailed in character. The first attempt by the federal government to obtain systematic financial statistics was initiated in 1832 when the House of Representatives passed a resolution directing the Secretary of the Treasury to collect state banking data on a yearly basis. The data were published beginning in 1833.[3] The data lack the detail of modern statistics, but include aggregate figures for deposits, notes, and holdings of specie, which are essential to the analysis of the demand and supply of money. It should be noted that the data are reported without explanation of the sources that were used to derive the series.

Aggregate financial data did not exist, until recently, for the period prior to 1833, with the only available information confined to personal observations and statements by various individuals which are at best quite sketchy and sometimes inconsistent.[4] In 1965, however, Van Fenstermaker (65) published an extensive and in depth analysis of the American commercial banking system up to 1837. This study provides a comprehensive source of early 19th century banking statistics in both aggregated and disaggregated form. These data were derived from intensive study of bank statements obtained from newspapers, periodicals and state archives. Throughout the monograph, Van Fenstermaker reports the relevant sources in a consistent manner and explains the assumptions and definitions involved in his analyses.

Thus, the aggregate financial data required to analyze the demand and supply of money in the early 1800's can be found in two different sources. The first, Van Fenstermaker's data, covers the years up to 1837 while the second, the Comptroller's data, is available for the period 1833 to 1862. Both of these sources are utilized in order to form a single series for variables specified in the money models. It should be noted that Van Fenstermaker's and the Comptroller's data are probably derived from different sources and thus are not consistent. In particular for the five years, 1833-1837, common to both sources, the series do not coincide. This problem has been discussed at length in several earlier studies.[5] In this study each banking series needed in the empirical work is constructed from Van Fenstermaker's data for the years up to and including 1833 and from the Comptroller's data for the period 1834 to 1859.[6] Van Fenstermaker's series do not contain data for the entire commercial banking sector, but the proportion of the total number of banks included in a given year is reported. Thus, on the assumption that the banks in the sample are representative of the entire bank population, Van Fenstermaker's figures are multiplied by the appropriate blowup factor in order to obtain series for the entire banking system. It should be noted that empirical tests were also conducted on series obtained by using Van Fenstermaker's data for the period through 1837 and the Comptroller's data for 1838 through 1859. The regression results, however, were almost identical, so that the conclusions reported in this study are not sensitive to the choice between the two data sources.

Throughout this study money is disaggregated into bank liabilities and currency in the hands of the public. Bank liabilites are the sum of demand deposits at commercial banks plus bank notes in circulation minus notes of other banks held within the banking system. These definitions correspond, as far as possible, to the contemporary definition of the money stock.[7] Temin (56) and Stevens (53) in their analyses of the financial statistics of the early 1800's derive series for the money supply which differ from that used in this study because, contrary to contemporary practice, net interbank balances are included.[8] If the data for the period were accurate, interbank balances should net to zero and there would be no differences between the money stock series used in this study and those of Temin and Stevens.[9]

The data for currency in the hands of the public are derived by subtracting bank holdings of specie from a series for the total specie in the United States. Official data for total specie from the year 1829 are published in the 1896 Report of the Comptroller of the Currency (63). This series, however, shows a suspiciously slow increase in specie compared to the additions in specie which can be calculated by netting domestic mining and specie exports and imports.[10] Consequently, a series for total specie is obtained by taking the Comptroller's estimate for specie in 1830 and adding the changes in specie calculated by subtracting specie exports from the sum of specie imports and mining. This is the series utilized in the empirical testing, although it should be noted that similar estimation results are obtained when the Comptroller's series is used.

Temin also reports a calculated series for currency, but his series is constructed improperly. Although currency and mining are year end figures while foreign trade flows are measured on a fiscal year basis, Temin merely adds them so that a calendar year figure is inappropriately paired with a fiscal year figure. Moreover, the definition of the fiscal year changed during the period so that for one year a trade flow figure which reflects six months is paired with a figure which measures the result of twelve months of mining. In order to rectify this problem for the series used in this study, twelve month calendar year trade figures are obtained by interpolation of the published figures. This yields a series which is characterized by a lower estimate of the level of total specie for each observation in the sample period than that calculated by Temin. Overall, by the end of the sample period this difference amounts to about 25 million dollars of specie.

APPENDIX B

In this appendix the problem of obtaining a yearly income series for the United States for the period 1823-1859 is analyzed. It is important to derive this series because income is a primary determinant of money demand. A yearly series constructed by Robert Gallman (21) is utilized for the years 1834-1859. Although decennial benchmarks are available for the years 1820 and 1830,[1] the problem is to obtain yearly estimates for the intervening years prior to 1834.

The simplest solution to this problem is to interpolate national income by assuming a smooth rate of growth for the years between the available data. Such a method, however, is clearly not efficient for two reasons. One, a large body of contemporary theory is available which specifies the determinants of income. Two, there exists a sizable body of data over the relevant period for many of the variables which determine income. Thus, given a body of theory and the appropriate data, an optimal, in the sense of minimum variance, "forecast" (or more properly a "midcast") of the missing observations for income can be obtained by utilizing an ordinary least squares regression.

Under the conditions of the classical linear model, it can be shown that ordinary least squares provides the best linear unbiased forecast.[2] It is assumed that the forecasted variable is a function of a linear combination of independent variables such that

$$Y_* = X_*'B + u_*$$

where Y_* are unknown values of the forecasted variable, X_* the known values of the independent variables, and u_* is a random disturbance with a finite variance which is independent of the sample disturbances. Thus,

$$Eu_* = 0$$

$$E(u_*^2) = \sigma^2$$

$$E(uu_*) = 0$$

where u is the vector of sample disturbances. If Y_* is forecasted by the ordinary least squares estimator, then

$$\hat{Y}_* = X_*'b$$

and the forecast error will be

$$f = Y_* - \hat{Y}_*$$

$$= X_*'B - X_*'b + u_*$$

or

$$= X_*'(B - b) + u_* \ .$$

The expected value of this error is

$$Ef = X_*'E(B - b) + Eu_*$$

and its variance is

$$\sigma_f^2 = Ef^2 = X_*'E(B - b)(B - b)'X_* + Eu_*^2$$

$$= X_*' \Sigma_{bb} X_* + \sigma^2$$

since

$$E(B - b)u_* = E(X'X)^{-1}X'uu_* = 0$$

and

$$Euu_* = 0 \ .$$

If this variance is to be a minimum, then it is clear that the sampling variance, $E(B - b)(B - b)'$, must be minimized. That is, the problem becomes one of finding the best linear unbiased estimator of the vector of true coefficients, B , from the available sample observations. Since only ordinary least squares minimizes this sampling variance, it follows that the best linear unbiased forecast of Y_* must in fact be

$$\hat{Y}_* = X_*'b$$

where $$b = (X'X)^{-1}X'Y$$

and $$E(B - b) = 0 .$$

The specification of an equation for midcasting income is based on the Keynesian theory of income determination. Thus, income, derived through a simple Keynesian multiplier relation, is viewed as a function of investment, government activity, and the foreign trade sector. Basically, the specification is

$$Y = f\ (\ I,\ G,\ T,\ X,\ M) \qquad (B.1)$$

where Y is income, I is investment, and G is government expenditures, T is taxes, X is exports, and M represents imports. In this model investment is viewed as exogenous, although in a larger model investment is often an endogenous variable functionally related to financial variables. This type of relationship, (B.1) is frequently used in analyses of income fluctuations in a modern context.[3]

A rival specification which has attracted much attention in contemporary literature assumes that income is basically a function of the money supply.[4] Such an equation, however, is not appropriate in this analysis because income is utilized as an explanatory variable for equations in which money is a dependent variable.

The technique of using a Keynesian autonomous expenditure equation to midcast missing observations for a series used as an independent variable in the money demand models, can be viewed as a form of instrumental variables. That is, the technique is the equivalent of replacing the unobservable income observations by a linear combination of exogenous instruments in order to explain money demand without introducing simultaneity. If income is explained as a function of the money stock, however, it would be impossible to assert the exogeneity of the instruments since the money stock is then effectively on both sides of the demand equation.

In such a case, simultaneity is clearly a severe problem.

Although no sophisticated system of national accounts existed for the period prior to the Civil War, a substantial number of series[5] is available which make it possible to estimate equation (B.1). Many series are found in The Historical Statistics of the United States (61), but in one instance no series exactly corresponds to a variable specified in equation (B.1). In such a case, the limitations of the data dictate the use of proxy variables. More specifically, there is no series for total investment in the early 1800's. Nevertheless, figures are available for both the production of vessels and the laying of railroad track which were two major components of investment. It is reasonable to assume that the capital costs of producing these forms of investment were relatively stable over the period and that investment in these forms of capital is probably highly correlated with other investment. Therefore these variables can serve as useful proxies for overall investment. An additional investment proxy for which a complete series is available is foreign investment.

Another variable that is used as a proxy to capture fluctuations in investment, is cotton production. Since cotton production was an extremely important sector of the American economy prior to the Civil War, it is reasonable to assume that during periods following profitable production of the crop, businessmen increased investment in order to meet expected increases in demand. This suggests an accelerator model in which investment is viewed as a simple function of cotton production.

$$I = f(C_{-1}) \qquad (B.2)$$

Cotton production is lagged one year since information about the harvested crop must have been required before investment plans were formulated. Alternatively, it can be hypothesized that businessmen sought to keep the level of their capital stocks, and also their output, consistent with the size of the cotton crop. This relationship is specified as

$$K = f(C_{-1})$$

or

$$K-K_{-1} = I = f(C_{-1} - C_{-2}) \qquad (B.3)$$

Thus in this case ,the lagged change in cotton production is the investment proxy entered in the income equation. Both equations (B.2) and (B.3) are subjected to empirical testing.

Few data problems emerge in obtaining series for government expenditures, G, and tax revenue, T, since in general accurate data were maintained for federal expenditures and receipts during the early 1800's. Although some analyses use the surplus or deficit,expenditures minus receipts, in order to obtain the net effect of government policy on income, in this case it is more appropriate to enter them separately. Since most government receipts were obtained from custom duties, it is reasonable to assume that federal taxation altered the level of income only slightly if at all.[6] The federal expenditures series excludes interest payments on the national debt which is standard practice in modern analyses since this is a transfer payment which does not alter the level of national income. In a study by Davis and Legler (13) figures are reported for state and local government revenues and expenditures on a regional per capita basis. These series are aggregated to the national level and are also used in the regressions in order to capture the effect of state and local government activity on income.

During the early 1800's perhaps the most accurate and certainly the most detailed data were collected for exports and imports. These two series are used with only minor adjustment.

The data series discussed above are the major variables specified in the national income equation. However, an additional variable, population, which grew at a rapid rate during the pre-Civil War period, is entered in the specification to allow for the possible effects of population growth on income. In general, higher birth rates lead to an increase in the number of children and hence an increase in the dependency ratio of children to adults. Consequently, an increase in population should lead to a higher marginal propensity to consume, a larger multiplier, and an increase in income. Since some of the increase in population during the early 1800's was due to a rise in the level of immigration, immigration is also tested as a variable in the income equation. Immigrants consisted primarily of adults so that the full population figures are likely to overstate the impetus to aggregate demand derived from population increases. Thus, given that population is included in the equation, the level of immigration should have a negative impact on income. It should be noted that a negative sign does not imply that an increase in immigration reduces income because immigration also has a positive effect on income through the population variable. It merely implies that an increase in immigration does not increase income as much as a similar natural population increase.

The estimation results for the income equation are reported in Table B.1. Each equation is estimated over the sample period 1834 through 1859 with the additional decennial benchmark years 1820 and 1830 included in the sample. Two alternative sets of benchmarks figures for the census years are available, those of Robert Martin (39) and Paul David (11). In general Martin's figures are unrealistically low and imply that real income did not grow as rapidly as population prior to 1830.[7] Consequently David's benchmarks, which imply an increase in real per capita GNP of about 1.5 percent per year for the period 1810 to 1830, are utilized in

Table B.1

Dependent Variable: Nominal GNP*

	I_f	V	RRD	C_{-1}	$C_{-1}-C_{-2}$	G_F	G_{SL}	G_C	X	N	IM	Constant	R^2/SE/DW
1)	.204	.227	.012	.176		1.110	.997		.361	5.003	-.213	-34.996	.99
	(1.48)	(4.42)	(1.73)	(1.20)		(2.58)	(1.79)		(2.10)	(2.72)	(-4.43)	(-1.99)	11.59
													2.33
2)	.229	.199	.014		.072	1.222	1.043		.413	5.116	-.201	-35.076	.99
	(1.65)	(2.83)	(1.97)		(.83)	(2.83)	(1.84)		(2.44)	(2.73)	(-4.26)	(-1.94)	11.83
													2.43
3)	.201	.228	.011	.176				1.066	.364	4.972	-.212	-35.316	.99
	(1.51)	(4.61)	(1.85)	(1.24)				(3.46)	(2.19)	(2.79)	(-4.58)	(-2.07)	11.29
													2.33
4)	.227	.201	.014		.071			1.153	.418	5.071	-.200	-35.645	.99
	(1.68)	(4.53)	(2.09)		(.83)			(3.79)	(2.55)	(2.80)	(-4.39)	(-2.04)	11.53
													2.43

*Sources: The Historical Statistics of the United States (61) is the source of the following variables used in the income regressions: merchant vessels built, p. 448; miles of railroad built, p. 428; foreign investment, p. 566; federal government high employment expenditures, p. 719; federal government receipts, p. 711; toatl exports and total imports (merchandise), p. 538; population, p. 7; and immigration, p. 57. When appropriate the series are adjusted so that the reporting dates are consistently on a calendar year basis. The series for the value of cotton production is calculated from Table 14 in Conrad and Meyer (70), p. 359. The series for state and local government expenditures and state and local government receipts are from Davis and Legler (13), p. 532.

the income regressions. Each regression is estimated by means of ordinary least squares. The t statistics are reported in parentheses below the estimated coefficients. The R^2, standard error in millions of dollars, and Durbin-Watson statistics are also reported for each equation.

The coefficients of two variables from the original specification are not reported in Table B.1 because they failed to have any statistical significance and were thus dropped from the final regressions. These variables are government receipts, at both the federal and state and local levels, and imports. It is not surprising that government receipts have little effect on income since custom duties constituted most of the government revenues. The imports variable had the wrong sign but the co-efficient had no statistical significance. This result suggests that imports failed to have a negative impact on income, perhaps because of foreign financing of these imports through capital exports to the United States.

Overall, the equations display similar properties. Each explains 99 percent of the variation in nominal GNP and has a small standard error of about 11.5 million dollars. Most of the variables have significant coefficients and each equation is characterized by an acceptable Durbin-Watson statistic.

In the first two equations, government expenditures are disaggregated into federal expenditure, G_F, and state and local expenditures, G_{SL}. In equation (1), C_{-1} is the investment proxy and in equation (2), $(C_{-1}-C_{-2})$ is used. Both equations yield essentially the same empirical results. The coefficients for the production of vessels, V, federal expenditures, exports, X, and population, N, are all positive as expected and significantly different from zero at the 5 percent level of significance. Also as expected, immigration, IM, has a negative coefficient which is small but strongly significant. This is consistent with the hypothesis that immigration does not increase aggregate demand as much as a similar natural increase in population. The coefficient for the federal expenditures variable is about 1.11. This is fairly small for a government expenditure multiplier by contemporary standards but for the early 1800's is surprisingly effective given that a large amount of government spending consisted of interest payments and transfer payments. State and local expenditures obtain a coefficient of .977 which is significant at the 10 percent level and is also a reasonable magnitude. Both foreign investment, I_f, and railroad investment, RRD, are positive although only the latter is significant at the 10 percent level. In equation (1) lagged cotton, (C_{-1}), is positive and has a t ratio of 1.2. Overall these results suggest that the primary investment variables in the equation are effective proxies for total investment. A similar result applies in equation (2) where the lagged change in cotton production, $(C_{-1}-C_{-2})$, is specified.

Since the coefficients for the federal and state and local expenditures variables are similar, equation (1) and (2) are reestimated with the two variables combined. This constrains both variables to have the same multiplier value. In equation (3), which specifies a lagged cotton production variable, the combined government expenditures variable, G_c, has a value of 1.066 with a t statistic of 3.46 while in equation (4), which contains the alternate cotton variable, the coefficient rises slightly to 1.153 with a t statistic of 3.79. The coefficient of the remaining variables have approximately the same values and t statistics obtained in equation (1) and (2).

Overall, each equation empirically explains fluctuations in income quite well and can satisfactorily serve to midcast the value of income for the years 1821-1829 and 1831-1833. Most of the variables are significant at the 10 percent level of significance or better. Moreover for many of these variables, a one tailed test can be justified because their sign, if different from zero, is known a priori. Thus most of these variables can be viewed as significant at the 5 percent level of significance. Each equation has a low standard error and each closely forecasts the benchmark years of 1820 and 1830. Equations (3) and (4) seem preferable, however, because more efficient estimates are obtained by constraining the multiplier coefficients for government expenditures to be equal. Equation (3) with the lagged level of cotton has a slightly lower standard error but equation (4) which specifies the lagged change in cotton, has a slightly better Durbin-Watson statistic.

The midcasted value for income for the years 1821-1829 and 1831-1833 for both equations (3) and (4) are reported in Appendix D along with the Gallman's decennial income figures. Both extrapolations are almost identical. When specified in the money demand equations developed in the text, both income series yield almost identical results. The results reported in the text utilize midcast values for income generated by equation (4) but these results are not sensitive to the choice of the midcasted income series.

APPENDIX C

American interest rate data for the pre-Civil War period are relatively sparse. Although Homer (31) details interest rate developments over the 19th century, there are only two interest rate series with any degree of completeness. These series are the United States government bond rate and the New England municipal bond rate. The former is particularly important for purposes of analyzing the demand for money since government bonds are viewed as a close substitute for money. Because of the absence of a well organized market for short term debt instruments in the pre-Civil War period, this pattern of substitution is particularly applicable.

A problem with the United States government bond rate series arises, however, because of the repayment of the national debt in 1832. Consequently no significant number of government bonds existed during the period 1833 to 1841 and therefore no government yields are available for those years. The purpose of this appendix is to analyze how to remedy this break in the data to obtain a consistent yield series.

Homer suggests that for this period the New England municipal rate best approximates market interest rate levels and trends.[1] A simple method of solving the problem of the break in the government bond series is to use these municipal bond rates for the missing years. It should be noted that although interest on contemporary municipal bonds is tax free which distorts their relation to other bond rates, this problem does not arise in the pre-Civil War period because of the absence of any federal income tax. Nevertheless, it is clear by inspection of the two series, which are graphed in Figure C.1., that the validity of such a procedure is doubtful. Although the series usually move together, they are at different levels which suggests that bondholders must have viewed these bonds as having different properties or degrees of risk. Thus it is inappropriate to substitute the municipal bond rate series for the missing federal bond rate observations.

An alternative procedure is to employ once again, an ordinary least squares regression in order to midcast the missing data for government bond rates. Since both government and municipal bonds are usually sold to the

Figure C.1

Long Term Interest Rates, 1801 - 1859*

* Source: Homer (31), pp. 286-287.

same set of bondholders, there must be a relationship between the two rates which can be captured by a regression. Any differences in risk or other factors are subsumed in the constant term. As demonstrated in the previous appendix, the midcast derived from such a regression is optimal in the sense of being unbiased and minimum variance. The results are contained in Table C.1. The sample period is 1805 to 1859, excluding the war years 1812 to 1815 and the period 1833 to 1841 which is to be midcasted.. The t statistics are reported in parentheses below the relevant coefficients. The R^2, standard error in percentage points and Durbin-Watson statistics[2] are also included.

The estimation results obtained for a simple specification of government bond rates, RL, on municipal bond rates, RMUN, are reported as equation (1). The findings indicate that the two rates are significantly related. Nevertheless the goodness of fit is relatively low with an R^2 of .43, which indicates that municipal bond rates alone are not quite as good an indicator of government bond rates as Homer suggests. Hence, alternate specifications are tested.

Table C.1

Dependent Variable: Long Term Government Bond Rate

	RMUN	RLUK	RGER	DUM	RCP	RCP_{-1}	RCP_{-2}	RCP_{-3}	Constant	R^2/SE	DW
1)	2.0230								-5.1155	.43	.22
	(5.91)								(-2.94)	.63	
2)		.9311							1.6092	.58	.68
		(7.94)							(3.55)	.54	
3)	1.3741	.7392							-4.6363	.76	.62
	(5.76)	(7.78)							(-4.08)	.40	
4)	1.2430	.6327	.1513	-1.0571					-3.3677	.79	.75
	(5.43)	(6.35)	(1.21)	(-1.72)					(-2.94)	.38	
5)					.0400	-.0301	-.1061		5.6298	.08	.49
					(.71)	(-.51)	(-1.80)		(8.45)	.61	
6)					.0347	-.0285	-.0914	-.0375	5.8573	.04	.48
					(.60)	(-.47)	(-1.41)	(-.62)	(7.55)	.63	

It is well known that contemporary international long term interest rates tend to be closely related to each other. The most sophisticated analysis of this problem has been carried out by Granger and Rees (27) who demonstrate that the spectral densities of international long term interest rates tend to be highly associated with each other. Consequently it is reasonable to hypothesize that a similar degree of association might be found between foreign interest rates and United States government bond rates for the pre-Civil War period. It is likely that the most relevant foreign interest rate for that period was the yield on long term British securities. This hypothesis is tested in equation (2) in which the United States government bond rate is specified as a function of the long term British rate, RLUK. The British rate coefficient is highly significant although the R^2 is still low, .58. Since the British rate and the municipal bond rate may capture different sources of variation, both variables are included in the specification and the results are reported as equation (3) and indicate a sharp improvement. Both variables are highly significant and the R^2 rises to .76. Thus, the regression successfully explains more than three quarters of the total variation in the government bond rate.

A variety of additional foreign interest rates[3] were also tested but without success. The only exception is a Prussian bond rate, RGER in equation (4), which has a positive coefficient but is not significant.[4] There is nevertheless, some improvement in the fit which might tentatively justify inclusion of the variable despite its lack of significance.

An alternative approach to explaining the govern- bond rate is also explored. There is a large literature which explains long term bond rates as a term structure of expected future short rates.[5] Empirically, expected rates are proxied by the use of past short term interest rates. Such equations have been estimated both for the United States and other nations and invariably display a striking ability to explain long term rates. Attempts to apply this analysis to the pre - Civil War period, however, indicate the lack of any significant relationship. Since no data on short term interest rates exists for the period prior to the 1830's, the term structure equation is estimated over the period 1842-1859. The estimation results are uniformly poor, as indicated by equations (5) and (6) in which several lags in the short term rate are utilized as independent variables. None of the lagged variables are significant and the adjusted R^2's are only .04 and .08 which indicate the inapplicability of a term structure theory to the pre-Civil War period. This result is not surprising, however, since the commercial paper market in the United States was not well organized until the post Civil War period.[6] During the early 1800's the commercial paper market was characterized by very sharp swings in interest rates with fluctuations of over 20 percentage points in almost every year.

Consequently, the midcasted values of the government bond rate series used in the text are obtained from the estimation results for equations (3) and (4) which relate the government bond rate to other long term rates. The midcasted values obtained from both equations are graphed in Figure C.2. These series can be interpreted as an estimate of the yield on federal government bonds that would have prevailed if government bonds were issued during the period 1833-1841. The two series are almost identical and produce essentially the same results when specified

Figure C.2

Estimates of the Government Bond Rate

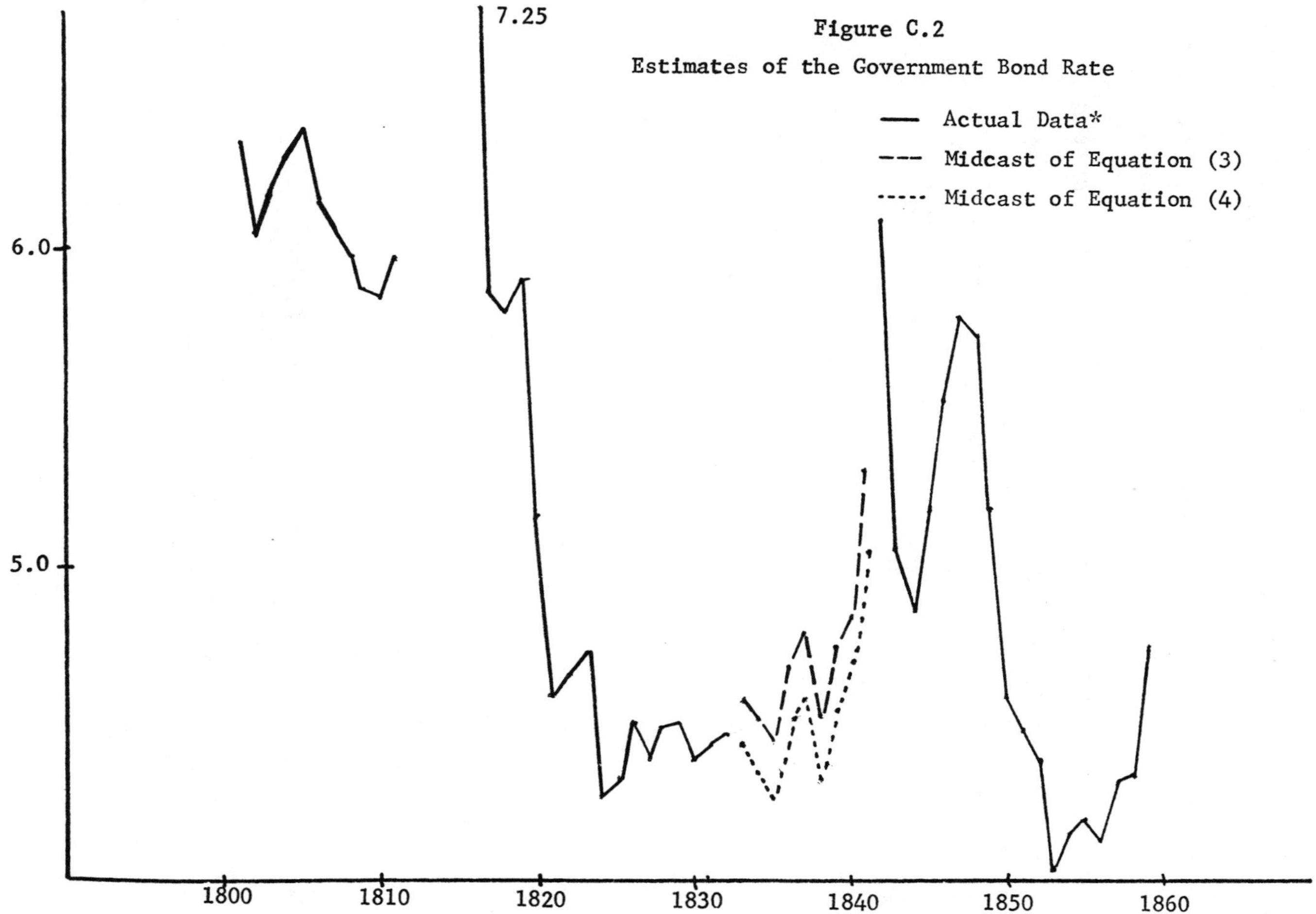

* Source: Homer (31), pp. 286-287.

in the demand for money equations. However, the empirical results reported in the text utilize the 1833-1841 values of the government bond rate that are midcasted by equation (3), which specifies only the municipal bond rate and the British long rate as independent variables.

APPENDIX D*

1823 - 1859

MD	Total Specie	MC	RL	RL_{ALT}	Y	Y_{ALT}
79.64	30.50	12.12	4.72	4.72	775.54	786.10
86.53	29.75	9.27	4.25	4.25	966.76	967.30
99.27	28.25	10.12	4.32	4.32	1000.03	1021.04
97.84	30.50	11.74	4.50	4.50	1019.33	1045.56
86.79	30.25	12.41	4.37	4.37	929.46	949.78
101.23	30.00	13.74	4.48	4.48	977.12	989.20
95.25	33.00	12.71	4.50	4.50	940.41	940.28
114.36	37.00	12.85	4.37	4.37	997.20	997.20
148.46	35.75	13.69	4.41	4.41	1072.71	1063.40
142.71	37.75	15.19	4.45	4.45	1277.75	1276.67
155.65	45.50	18.31	4.58	4.42	1376.84	1378.99
193.28	59.25	15.31	4.51	4.34		
249.69	67.56	27.54	4.43	4.26		
240.05	75.84	37.93	4.66	4.46		
175.87	82.67	47.49	4.77	4.56		
198.04	92.67	47.54	4.51	4.32		
161.87	90.15	57.04	4.74	4.52		
146.54	89.39	54.58	4.82	4.59	1643.60	1643.60
126.71	86.01	57.57	5.30	5.02		
101.43	93.15	59.63	6.07	6.07		
148.05	108.35	58.45	5.03	5.03		
165.59	107.49	63.25	4.85	4.85		
190.55	106.50	63.49	5.16	5.16		
184.20	119.14	84.00	5.50	5.50		
215.30	126.52	80.15	5.77	5.77		
193.21	132.03	88.41	5.71	5.71		
224.65	171.03	125.65	5.16	5.16		
266.93	207.53	158.86	4.58	4.58	2380.00	2380.00
271.04	232.03	184.12	4.47	4.47		
261.20	262.01	214.87	4.39	4.39		
370.22	298.50	239.09	4.02	4.02		
353.92	313.98	260.04	4.14	4.14		
383.68	320.49	261.17	4.18	4.18		
417.01	325.99	267.64	4.11	4.11		
328.69	335.99	261.58	4.30	4.30		
434.02	341.49	236.96	4.32	4.32		
441.40	334.50	250.91	4.72	4.74		

*All variables are in millions of dollars except interest rates which are in percentage points.

The data sources for this Appendix are as follows. Explanations for the series MD, total specie, and MC are found in Appendix A. Explanations for the series RL and RL_{ALT} are found in Appendix C. The series for Y and Y_{ALT} are explained in Appendix D. The decennial benchmarks for the income series can be found in Gallman (67), p. 26. The remaining income observations for the period 1834-1859 were obtained through private correspondence with Robert Gallman.

GLOSSARY

BR	Borrowed reserves
BS	Bank specie
C	Value of cotton production at New Orleans prices
DUM	Dummy variable
ER	Excess reserves
FR	Free reserves
G_C	Combined Federal government high employment expenditures and state and local government expenditures
G_F	Federal government high employment expenditures
G_{SL}	State and local government expenditures
HP	High powered money
i	Open market interest rates
I	Investment
I_f	Foreign investment
IM	Immigration
K	Physical capital stock
MC	Currency in the hands of the public
MD	Bank liabilities: notes and deposits

MD*	The maximum quantity of bank liabilities which can be supported by the given quantity of reserves.
MR	Minimum reserves
N	Population
PDOT	The rate of change in prices; approximated by P/P_{-1} in logarithmic form.
r	Commercial bank deposit rate
RCP	Commercial paper rate
PGER	Long term Prussian bond rate
RL	Long term government bond rate
RLUK	Long term British bond rate
RMUN	New England municipal bond rate
RR	Required reserves
RRD	Miles of railroad built
TR	Total reserves
UR	Unborrowed reserves
V	Merchant vessels built
X	Total exports
Z_D	Reserve requirement on bank liabilities
Y	Gross national product

FOOTNOTES

Chapter 2

1. An important example of how serious this can be is illustrated by Temin's derivation of a total currency series from government export, import and mining data for specie. When the fiscal years are properly matched and accounted for, the total series is lowered by more than $25 million dollars by the end of the pre- Civil War period. Moreover, a much smoother series results. See Temin (56), pp. 186-187 and Appendix D.

2. See Temin (56). Temin's reserve ratio is calculated as the ratio of bank specie to the total money supply. Since this definition of money includes currency in the hands of the public, this ratio reflects the interaction of the public's demand for both currency and bank liabilities as well as commercial bank behavior. Thus it is impossible to draw any conclusions about commercial bank behavior on the basis of patterns in this ratio.

Chapter 3

1. The empirical literature on money demand is large, but among the most important contributions are Brunner (6), Meltzer (40), Lee (36), Laidler (34), and Latané (35). See Laidler (33) for a comprehensive survey of this literature.

2. The foremost of these economists is I.Fisher (16).

3. See Pigou (45), Latané (35).

4. Keynes (32).

5. A thin capital market means that it is difficult to buy or sell a substantial quantity of the asset on short notice without sharp price changes.

6. Among the most important contributions to this literature are Tobin (58), Baumol (3),Tobin (59),and Friedman (17). The first two citations refer to the development of inventory models, while the latter two derive the demand for money from portfolio considerations.

7. This modification usually characterizes modern empirical work involving quarterly data but is less common in analyses employing annual data. For example, see the work of Goldfeld (23), de Leeuw (14), Modigliani, Rasche,and Cooper(43), Chow (9), and Slovin and Sushka (52).

8. This is done, for example, by Modigliani, Rasche, and Cooper (43).

9. See Goldberger (22), pp. 255-258.

10. See especially the writing of Milton Friedman (18).

11. For a discussion of the data problems, see Appendix A.

12. Such a practice is uniformly applied in contemporary empirical studies. For example, most econometric work excludes not only the war years of the 1940's and early 1950's, but also the Depression years of the 1930's.

13. See Brunner (6), Meltzer (40), Friedman (18), Latané (35), for discussions of this problem.

14. See Goldfeld (23), pp. 78-79; Modigliani, Rasche, and Cooper (43), pp. 166-167, and Slovin and Sushka (52).

15. For a summary of these arguments see Goldfeld (23), p. 79. Also see Cagan (7), pp. 312-15.

16. For details about the data definitions and the construction of these two dependent variables, see Appendix A.

17. Cochrane and Orcutt (10).

18. Throughout the paper, the t statistics are considered to be significantly different from zero if they lie outside a 95 percent confidence interval about zero.

19. Details about the income series can be found in Apprendix B.

20. All regressions were also estimated in real terms but the results were very similar and thus are not reported.

21. For an explanation of the techniques utilized in order to supply the missing observations in this series, see Appendix C.

22. This short term rate series is only available beginning in 1831 and therefore inclusion of a dummy variable is required when RCP is specified in the regressions.

23. The size of the income elasticity of the demand for money has been a topic of frequent discussions in contemporary literature. Overall, most economists believe that this elasticity is close to unity. See Laidler (33), p.107, and Poole (46), pp. 486-493.

24. Usually the speed of adjustment, estimated for quarterly data, ranges between 10 and 20 percent per quarter which is generally considered to be fairly slow; e.g., see Modigliani, Rasche and Cooper (43), p. 173. However, faster speeds of adjustment have been reported by Slovin and Sushka (52), pp. 6-8.

25. The long run elasticity is defined as b/λ where b is the estimated short run elasticity and λ is the speed of adjustment, where $(1-\lambda)$ is the coefficient of the lagged dependent variable.

26. This is not a surprising result since there is no evidence in the contemporary money demand literature that the demand for money is affected by price expectations. See for example Friedman (17), Selden (49), Goldfeld (24), pp. 607-713.

27. Goldfeld (23) , pp. 79-81 hypothesizes such a result and finds empirical support in his currency and demand deposit equations when specified in non logarithmic form. In his logarithmic equations, however, the income elasticity for currecy exceeds that of demand deposits.

28. See, for example, Goldfeld (23), pp. 80-81, and Modigliani, Rasche and Cooper (43), pp. 177-179.

Chapter 4

1. There were a few cases of state imposed reserve requirements. For example, Louisiana adopted such regulations but only in 1842. See Green (68), p. 201.

2. It is assumed in this analysis that reserves are only held against demand deposits. In the modern context, the Federal Reserve also requires banks to hold reserves on time deposits. This factor can easily be added to the analysis, but it would complicate the derivation without affecting the results. For an example of such an analysis, see Slovin and Sushka (51),p. 7.

3. See Modigliani, Rasche, and Cooper (43), pp. 191-193, and Hendershott and deLeeuw (30),pp. 600-601.

4. This formulation is standard in the recent literature. See for example, Branson (5), pp. 258-260, and Modigliani, Rasche, and Cooper (43), p. 188. The original exposition of this new view is found in Tobin (57), and Tobin and Brainard (60).

5. See Van Fenstermaker (65), pp. 43-53, for a description of bank asset portfolios during the early 1800's. For contemporary analyses of bank portfolio behavior, see Goldfeld (23).

6. As noted earlier, total specie is considered to be exogenous since it is assumed to be unaffected by commercial bank behavior in the short run. In a more extensive model this variable could be treated as an endogenous function of mining, technical progress, and the international specie flow mechanism. Such an analysis, however is beyond the scope of this study.

7. This question has been the subject of a long historical debate by researchers, but it is not a key issue in this study. For a review and analysis of this debate, see Temin (56), pp. 44-48.

8. See Teigen (55) for the original statement of the endogenous money supply formulation. A more general discussion is found in Branson (5), p. 262.

9. The R^2's should not be compared to the R^2's obtained for the supply regressions in which the level of demand deposits is specified as the dependent variable. In Teigen's money supply work the R^2's were in the range of .70 (55), pp. 64.

10. It is interesting to note that during the period 1823-1859 the income velocity of money fell gradually from 8.45 in 1823 to 6.05 in 1859. These results are consistent with Friedman and Schwartz (20) who estimate velocity in 1869 to be about five. This secular decline in velocity continued until the 1940's.

Chapter 5

1. The list of references which discuss the traditional view is long. Some of the best known works are Hammond (29), Meyers (42), Schlesinger (48). The clearest statement of the new view is Temin (56); also see Macesich (37).

2. To provide a more efficient estimate of the remaining parameters, the equation is reestimated omitting the interest rate variable. The results are reported as equation (1c). This procedure is applied throughout this section whenever an interest rate coefficient is not significant or has an incorrect sign.

3. Both the traditional historical view of the Bank War and the newer version assert conclusions which primarily deal with the effect of the Bank War on bank behavior. Thus, the stability of the money supply function is particularly important.

4. See Rockoff (47), pp. 454-456; Hammond (29), pp. 627-630; and Studenskii and Kroos (54), p. 107.

5. Recent work by Barro and Santomero (2) has sought to develop contemporary time series data for the rate of return on demand deposits by utilizing information on bank service charges.

6. See Van Fenstermaker (65), pp. 36-38.

7. This holds as long as $(ik-r) > 0$, that is the intermediary does not operate at a loss. In the linear case, the derivative is equal to exactly one half.

8. This procedure is commonly used in modern econometric analyses in order to evaluate the stability of functional relationships. This technique is employed, for example, by Eckstein and Brinner (15), pp. 24-25, in an analysis of the Phillips Curve and Goldfeld (24), pp. 589-590, in his study of money demand. A more sophisticated technique has recently been proposed by Goldfeld and Quandt (26) in which the data are allowed to determine the switching of the specification. No published results have yet appeared which actually apply this technique. An alternative technique for evaluating stability is the use of the Chow test (69) which provides a means of testing whether sets of coefficients are significantly different from each other. Because the evidence clearly indicates that there are two different specifications for the two different subperiods, the desirability of the Chow test is limited.

9. Once again the reported results are for ordinary least squares regressions. When the Cochrane-Orcutt technique is utilized, the results for the estimated serial correlation coefficient often fail to converge.

10. These policies include 1) the distribution of government surplus to the states in 1836; 2) the prohibition of note issuance in denominations of less than five dollars by state banks holding government deposits in 1836; and 3) the Specie Circular of 1836 which required the purchase price of public lands to be paid in specie.

11. Under the international gold standard, imbalances in foreign trade were rectified through the transmission of specie from deficit to surplus nations. The outflow of gold from the deficit country induced a contraction in the money supply, deflation and a rise in the exchange rate, while the inflow of specie to surplus nations produced an expansion in the money supply, inflation, and a decline in the exchange rate. Thus, the imbalance in foreign trade is counteracted. For a general discussion, see Blaug (4), pp. 135-137.

12. It is not clear that such policies would have been carried out by a central bank. For example, in a similar situation during the early 1930's, the Federal Reserve actually sought to reduce the quantity of high powered money which intensified the economic crisis. See Friedman and Schwartz (20).

Appendix A

1. Much of the responsibility for collection and publication of financial data was assumed by the Federal Reserve with its establishment in 1913.

2. The classic work in this area is Friedman and Schwartz (20). Most other financial research has been confined to the twentieth century and particularly to the period after the establishment of the Federal Reserve System.

3. These statistics are known as the Comptroller's data, which exist in published form in only a few sources: Executive Documents, 1892-1893 (64), pp. 84-85; Report of the Comptroller of the Currency, 1876 (62), pp. LXXXIII, XCIVXCV; also Report of the Comptroller of the Currency, 1896 (63), p. 544.

4. For a description of this situation, see the Report of the Comptroller 1876, (62), pp. XXXVIIIff.

5. See the Appendix in Temin (56) for a lengthy discussion of this topic. Also see Stevens (53).

6. Although the Comptroller's series report statistics for 1833, these figures were not used because of several apparent errors in a few of the series, especially for specie.

7. In contemporary analyses the components of the narrowly defined money stock, M1, are demand deposits of commercial banks other than interbank and government deposits plus currency in the hands of the public.

8. An important reason for excluding interbank balances is that distortions may result when Van Fenstermaker's sample data are blown up for the early period.

9. Actually there would be a difference with Steven's series because he subtracts specie funds held by banks on the grounds that they may have consisted primarily of notes of other banks. Temin considers specie funds instead, as merely short term, liquid loans.

10. Data for mining and exports and imports of specie are reported in the Historical Statistics of the United States (61), pp. 371, 538.

Appendix B

1. See David (1) and Martin (39).

2. The following derivation is drawn from Goldberger (22), pp. 169-170.

3. See especially, Ando and Modigliani (1).

4. See Friedman and Meiselman (19).

5. These series are characterized by discrepancies in reporting dates which must be rectified in order to provide an appropriate series. This problem is identical to the difficulties in deriving the currency series, as described in Appendix A.

6. See Davis and Legler (13), 516.

7. In general, economic historians have rejected the validity of Martin's benchmarks. For example, see David (11), pp. 153-153.

Appendix C

1. Homer (31), p. 302.

2. Because of the break in the series, the standard Durbin-Watson statistic is not valid.

3. Various interest rates for France, Germany, and Holland were tested. See Homer (31), pp. 216-273.

4. A dummy variable is specified in the regression because of gaps in the Prussian interest rate series.

5. A summary of this literature is found in Malkiel (38), pp. 178-197.

6. See Lance Davis (12).

BIBLIOGRAPHY

1. Ando, Albert and Franco Modigliani. "The Relative Stability of Monetary Velocity and the Investment Multiplier." American Economic Review, Vol.55, No. 4 (September 1965), pp. 693-728.

2. Barro, Robert and Anthony Santomero. "Household Money Holdings and the Demand Deposit Rate." Journal of Money Credit and Banking, Vol. 4, No. 2 (May 1972), pp. 397-413.

3. Baumol, William. "The Transactions Demand for Cash-An Inventory Theoretic Approach." Quarterly Journal of Economics, Vol. 66, No. 4 (November 1952), pp. 545-556.

4. Blaug, Mark. Economic Theory in Retrospect. Homewood, Illinois; Richard Irwin, 1968.

5. Branson, William. Macroeconomic Theory and Policy. New York: Harper and Row, 1972.

6. Brunner, Karl. "Some Further Evidence on Supply and Demand Functions for Money. Journal of Finance, Vol. 19, No. 2 (May 1964), pp. 240-283.

7. Cagan, Phillip. " The Demand for Currency Relative to the Total Money Supply." Journal of Political Economy, Vol. 66, No. 4 (August 1958), pp. 303-328.

8. Chandler, Lester. The Economics of Money and Banking. New York: Harper and Row, 1973.

9. Chow, Gregory. "On the Long Run and Short Run Demand for Money." Journal of Political Economy, Vol. 74, No. 2 (April 1966), pp. 111-131.

10. Cochrane, D. and G. Orcutt. "Application of Least Squares Regression to Relationships Containing Autocorrelated Errors." Journal of the American Statistical Association. Vol. 44, No. 1 (March 1949), pp. 32-61.

11. David, Paul. "The Growth of Real Product in the United States Before 1840: New Evidence, Controlled Conjectures." Journal of Economic History, Vol. 27, No. 2 (June 1967), pp. 151-197.

12. Davis, Lance. "Capital Mobility and American Growth" in Robert Fogel and Stanley Engerman, editors, The Reinterpretation of American Economic History. New York: Harper and Row, 1971.

13. Davis, Lance and John Legler. "The Government in the American Economy, 1815-1905: A Quantitative Study." Journal of Economic History, Vol. 26, No. 4 (December 1966), pp. 514-552.

14. deLeeuw, Frank. "A Model of Financial Behavior." in James S. Duesenberry et. al., editors, The Brookings Quarterly Econometric Model of the United States. Chicago: Rand McNally, 1965.

15. Eckstein, Otto and Roger Brinner. "The Inflation Process in the United "States." A Study prepared for the use of the Joint Economic Committee, U.S.Congress, 92nd Congress, 2nd Session, Washington, D.C.: U.S. Government Printing Office, 1972.

16. Fisher, Irving. The Rate of Interest. New York: MacMillan and Co., 1930.

17. Friedman , Milton. "The Demand for Money, Some Theoretical and Empirical Results." Journal of Political Economy. Vol. 67, No. 3 (June 1959), pp. 327-351.

18. Friedman , Milton, (ed). Studies in the Quantity Theory of Money. Chicago: University of Chicago Press, 1956.

19. Friedman, Milton and David Meiselman. "The Relative Stability of Monetary Velocity and the Investment Multiplier in the United States, 1897-1958," in Commission on Money and Credit, _Stabilization Policies_. Englewood Cliffs: Prentice Hall, 1963.

20. Friedman, Milton and Anna Schwartz. _A Monetary History of the United States 1867-1960_. Princeton: Princeton University Press, 1963.

21. Gallman, Robert. Private Correspondence.

22. Goldberger, Arthur. _Econometric Theory._ New York: John Wiley, 1964.

23. Goldfeld, Stephen. _Commercial Bank Behavior and Economic Activity_. Amsterdam; North Holland, 1966.

24. Goldfeld, Stephen. "The Demand for Money Revisited." _Brookings Papers on Economic Activity_, Vol. 3, No. 3 (1973), pp. 577-643.

25. Goldfeld, Stephen and Dwight Jaffee. "The Determinants of Deposit Rate Setting by Savings and Loan Associations." _Journal of Finance_, Vol. 25, No. 3 (June 1970), pp. 615-632.

26. Goldfeld, Stephen and Richard Quandt. "A Markov Model for Switching Regressions." _Journal of Econometrics_, Vol.1, No. 1 (March 1973), pp. 3-16.

27. Granger, C.W. and H.J. Rees. "Spectral Analysis of the Term Structure of Interest Rates." _Review of Economic Studies_, Vol. 35, No. 101 (January 1968). pp. 67-76.

28. Griliches, Zvi. "Distributed Lags: A Survey." _Econometrica_, Vol. 35, No. 1 (January 1967), pp. 16-49.

29. Hammond, Bray. _Banks and Politics in America From the Revolution to the Civil War._ Princeton: Princeton Univertiy Press, 1957.

30. Hendershott, Patric and Frank deLeeuw. "Free Reserves, Interest Rates and Deposits: A Synthesis." _Journal of Finance,_ Vol. XXV, No. 3 (June 1970), pp. 599-613.

31. Homer, Sidney. _A History of Interest Rates._ New Brunswick: Rutgers University Press, 1963.

32. Keynes, John M. _The General Theory of Employment, Interest, and Money_. New York: Harcourt, Brace, 1936 .

33. Laidler, David. _The Demand for Money: Theories and Evidence_. Scranton, Pennsylvania: International Textbook Co. , 1969.

34. Laidler, David. "Some Evidence on the Demand for Money." _Journal of Political Economy_, Vol. 74, No. 1 (February 1966), pp. 55-68.

35. Latané, Henry. "Cash Balances and the Interest Rate - A Pragmatic Approach." _Review of Economics and Statistics,_ Vol. 36, No. 4 (November 1954), pp. 456-460.

36. Lee, Tong. "Alternative Interest Rates and the Demand for Money: The Empirical Evidence." _American Economic Review_, Vol. 57, No. 5 (December 1967), pp. 1168-1181.

37. Macesich, George. "Sources of Monetary Disturbances in the U.S., 1834-1835." _Journal of Economic History_, Vol. 20, No. 3 (September 1960), pp. 407-434.

38. Malkiel, Burton. _The Term Structure of Interest Rates: Expectations and Behavior Patterns,_ Princeton: Princeton University Press, 1966.

39. Martin, Robert. _National Income in the United States, 1799-1938._ New York: National Industrial Conference Board, 1939.

40. Meltzer, Allan. "The Demand for Money: The Evidence from the Time Series." Journal of Political Economy, Vol. 71, No. 3 (June 1963), pp. 219-246.

41. Meyer, Paul. "Comment." Journal of Finance, Vol. 33, No. 4 (September 1967), pp. 467-470.

42. Meyers, Marvin. The Jacksonian Persuasion. Stanford: Stanford University Press, 1960.

43. Modigliani, Franco, Robert Rasche and J. Phillip Cooper. "Central Bank Policy, The Money Supply and the Short Term Rate of Interest". Journal of Money, Credit and Banking, Vol. 2, No. 2 (May 1970), pp. 166-218.

44. Payne, Peter and Lance Davis. The Savings Bank of Baltimore, 1818-1866: A Historical and Analytical Study. Baltimore: Johns Hopkins Press, 1956.

45. Pigou, A.C. " The Value of Money." Quarterly Journal of Economics, Vol. 37, (November 1917), pp. 36-65.

46. Poole, William. "Whither Money Demand?" Brookings Papers on Economic Activity. Vol. 1, No. 3 (1970), pp. 485-500.

47. Rockoff, Hugh. "Money, Prices and Banks in the Jacksonian Era," in Robert Fogel and Stanley Engerman, editors, The Reinterpretation of American Economic History. New York: Harper and Row, 1971.

48. Schlesinger, Arthur. The Age of Jackson. Boston: Little, Brown, 1945.

49. Selden, Richard. "Monetary Velocity in the United States," in Milton Friedman (ed.), Studies in the Quantity Theory of Money. Chicago: Chicago University Press, 1956.

50. Slovin, Myron B. "Deposit Rate Setting at Financial Institutions," in Edward Gramlich and Dwight Jaffee, editors. Savings Deposits, Mortgages, and Housing. Lexington, Massachusetts: D.C. Heath, 1972.

51. Slovin, M.B. and M.E. Sushka. "The Macroeconomic Impact of Changes in the Ceilings on Deposit Rates." Unpublished paper, Board of Governors of the Federal Reserve System, 1974.

52. Slovin, M.B. and M.E. Sushka. "The Structural Shift in the Demand for Money." Unpublished paper, Board of Governors of the Federal Reserve System, 1973.

53. Stevens, Edward. "Composition of the Money Stock Prior to the Civil War." Journal of Money, Credit and Banking, Vol. 3, No. 1 (February 1971), pp. 84-101.

54. Studenskii, Paul and Herman Kroos. Financial History of the United States. New York: McGraw Hill, 1963.

55. Teigen, Ronald. "The Demand for and Supply of Money" in Ronald Teigen and Warren Smith, editors, Money, National Income, and Stabilization Policy Homewood, Illinois; Richard Irwin and Co., 1965.

56. Temin, Peter. The Jacksonian Economy. New York: W.W. Norton, 1969.

57. Tobin, James. "Commercial Banks as 'Creators' of Money", in Deane Carson, editor, Banking and Monetary Studies. Homewood, Illinois: Richard Irwin, 1963.

58. Tobin, James. "The Interest Elasticity of Transactions Demand for Cash." Review of Economics and Statistics, Vol. 38 (August 1956), pp. 241-247.

59. Tobin, James. "Liquidity Preference as Behavior Towards Risk." Review of Economic Studies, Vol. 25, No. 1 (February 1958), pp. 65-88.

60. Tobin, James and William Brainard. "Financial Intermediaries and the Effectivess of Monetary Controls." American Economic Review, Vol. 53, No. 2 (May 1963), pp. 383-400.

61. U.S. Bureau of the Census. Historical Statistics of the United States, Colonial Times to 1957. Washington, D.C.: Government Printing Office, 1960.

62. U.S. Treasury Department. Annual Report of the Comptroller of the Currency, 1876. Washington, D.C.: Government Printing Office, 1876.

63. U.S. Treasury Department. Annual Report of the Comptroller of the Currency, 1896, 2 Vols. Washington, D.C.: Government Printing Office, 1896.

64. U.S. Treasury Department. The Executive Documents, 1892-1893, Vol. 5. Washington, D.C.: Government Printing Office, 1893.

65. Van Fenstermaker, J. The Development of American Commercial Banking, 1782-1837. Kent, Ohio: Kent State University, 1965.

66. Weber, Gerald S. "Interest Rates on Mortgages and Dividend Rates on Savings and Loan Shares." Journal of Finance, Vol. 21, No. 3 (September 1966), pp. 515-521.

67. Gallman, Robert E. "Gross National Product in the United States, 1834-1909" in Output, Employment and Productivity in the United States after 1800. Studies in Income and Wealth, Vol. 30. New York: Columbia University Press for the National Bureau of Economic Research, 1966.

68. Green, George D. "Louisiana 1804-1861" Chapter 4 in Rondo Cameron, ed., Banking and Economic Development: Some Lessons in History. New York: Oxford University Press, 1972.

69. Chow, Gregory C. "Tests for Equality between Sets of Coefficients in Two Linear Regressions." Econometrica, Vol. 28, No.3 (July 1960), pp. 591-605.

70. Conrad, Alfred and John Meyer. "The Economics of Slavery in the Ante-Bellum South" in Robert Fogel and Stanley Engerman, editors, The Reinterpretation of American Economic History. New York: Harper and Row, 1971.

71. Myers, Margaret G. The New York Money Market, Vol. 1. New York: Columbia University Press, 1931.

72. Smith, Walter B. and Arthur H. Cole. Fluctuations in American Business 1790-1860. Cambridge : Harvard University Press, 1935.

Dissertations in American Economic History

An Arno Press Collection

1978 Publications

Alston, Richard Moss. **Commercial Irrigation Enterprise, the Fear of Water Monopoly, and the Genesis of Market Distortion in the Nineteenth Century American West.** (Doctoral Thesis, Cornell University, 1970). 1978

Buss, Dietrich G. **Henry Villard.** (Revised Doctoral Dissertation, Claremont Graduate School, 1976). 1978

Chernow, Barbara Ann. **Robert Morris: Land Speculator, 1790-1801.** (Doctoral Dissertation, Columbia University, 1974). 1978

Cranmer, H. Jerome. **The New Jersey Canals.** (Doctoral Dissertation, Columbia University, 1955). 1978

Dick, Trevor J. O. **An Economic Theory of Technological Change.** (Revised Doctoral Dissertation, University of Washington, 1970). 1978

Eis, Carl. **The 1919-1930 Merger Movement in American Industry.** (Doctoral Dissertation, The City University of New York, 1968). 1978

Esbitt, Milton. **International Capital Flows and Domestic Economic Fluctuation.** (Doctoral Thesis, Michigan State University, 1970). 1978

Godfrey, John Munro. **Monetary Expansion in the Confederacy.** Doctoral Dissertation, University of Georgia, 1976). 1978

Golembe, Carter H. **State Banks and the Economic Development of the West, 1830-44.** (Doctoral Dissertation, Columbia University, 1952). 1978

Govan, Thomas Payne. **Banking and the Credit System in Georgia, 1810-1860.** (Doctoral Thesis, Vanderbilt University, 1937). 1978

Gray, Jean Mathieson. **The Term Structure of Interest Rates in the United States: 1884-1914.** (Doctoral Dissertation, University of California, Berkeley, 1969). 1978

Heavner, Robert Owen. **Economic Aspects of Indentured Servitude in Colonial Pennsylvania, 1771-1773.** (Doctoral Dissertation, Stanford University, 1976). 1978

Herbst, Lawrence A. **Interregional Commodity Trade from the North to the South and American Economic Development in the Antebellum Period.** (Doctoral Dissertation, University of Pennsylvania, 1974). 1978

Klepper, Robert. **The Economic Bases for Agrarian Protest Movements in the United States, 1870-1900.** (Doctoral Dissertation, University of Chicago, 1973). 1978

Kline, Mary-Jo. **Gouverneur Morris and the New Nation, 1775-1788.** (Doctoral Dissertation, Columbia University, 1970). 1978

Koller, Roland H., II. **Predatory Pricing in a Market Economy.** (Doctoral Dissertation, University of Wisconsin, 1969). 1978

Lavin, Marilyn Anne. **William Bostwick.** (Doctoral Dissertation, Columbia University, 1977). 1978

Lee, Ronald Demos. **Econometric Studies of Topics in Demographic History.** (Doctoral Thesis, Harvard University, 1970). 1978

Leet, Don R., **Population Pressure and Human Fertility Response.** (Doctoral Dissertation, University of Pennsylvania, 1972). 1978

Libecap, Gary D. **The Evolution of Private Mineral Rights.** (Doctoral Dissertation, University of Pennsylvania, 1976). 1978

MacDowell, Michael Alan. **Public Understanding of Economic Policies.** (Doctoral Dissertation, Ball State University, 1974). 1978

Miller, Randall M. **The Cotton Mill Movement in Antebellum Alabama.** (Doctoral Dissertation, Ohio State University, 1971). 1978

Morrison, Grant. **Isaac Bronson and the Search for System in American Capitalism, 1789-1838.** (Doctoral Dissertation, The City University of New York, 1973). 1978

Munyon, Paul Glenn. **A Reassessment of New England Agriculture in the Last Thirty Years of the Nineteenth Century.** (Revised Doctoral Dissertation, Harvard University, 1975). 1978

Perry, Joseph McGarity. **The Impact of Immigration on Three American Industries, 1865-1914.** (Doctoral Dissertation, Northwestern University, 1966). 1978

Ready, Milton L. **The Castle Builders.** (Revised Doctoral Dissertation, University of Georgia, 1970). 1978

Soper, John Charles. **The Long Swing in Historical Perspective.** (Doctoral Dissertation, University of Massachusets, 1970). 1978

Spencer, Austin H. **An Examination of Relative Downward Industrial Price Flexibility, 1870-1921.** (Doctoral Thesis, Indiana University, 1972). 1978

Sushka, Marie Elizabeth. **An Economic Model of the Money Market in the United States, 1823-1859.** (Doctoral Dissertation, University of Georgia, 1974). 1978

Synnott, Thomas Whitney, III. **Investment Policies, Growth and Profitability in the New England Cotton Textile Industry, 1830-1914.** (Doctoral Dissertation, Yale University, 1968). 1978

Vatter, Harold G. **Some Aspects of the Problem of Small Enterprise As Seen in Four Selected Industries.** (Doctoral Dissertation, University of California, Berkeley, 1950). 1978

Wilkenfeld, Bruce Martin. **The Social and Economic Structure of the City of New York, 1695-1796.** (Doctoral Dissertation, Columbia University, 1973). 1978

Womack, Roy Douglas. **An Analysis of the Credit Controls of the Second Bank of the United States.** (Doctoral Dissertation, University of Alabama, 1971). 1978

Xander, James Allen. **Vault Cash and the Role of Commercial Banks in Regional Economic Development—United States, 1870-1913.** (Doctoral Dissertation, University of Georgia, 1974). 1978

1977 Publications

Ankli, Robert Eugene. **Gross Farm Revenue in Pre-Civil War Illinois.** (Doctoral Dissertation, University of Illinois, 1969). 1977

Asher, Ephraim. **Relative Productivity, Factor-Intensity and Technology in the Manufacturing Sectors of the U.S. and the U.K. During the Nineteenth Century.** (Doctoral Dissertation, University of Rochester, 1969). 1977

Campbell, Carl. **Economic Growth, Capital Gains, and Income Distribution:** 1897-1956. (Doctoral Dissertation, University of California at Berkeley, 1964). 1977

Cederberg, Herbert R. **An Economic Analysis of English Settlement in North America, 1583-1635.** (Doctoral Dissertation, University of California at Berkeley, 1968). 1977

Dente, Leonard A. **Veblen's Theory of Social Change.** (Doctoral Dissertation, New York University, 1974). 1977

Dickey, George Edward. **Money, Prices and Growth;** The American Experience, 1869-1896. (Doctoral Dissertation, Northwestern University, 1968). 1977

Douty, Christopher Morris. **The Economics of Localized Disasters:** The 1906 San Francisco Catastrophe. (Doctoral Dissertation, Stanford University, 1969). 1977

Harper, Ann K. **The Location of the United States Steel Industry, 1879-1919.** (Doctoral Dissertation, Johns Hopkins University, 1976). 1977

Holt, Charles Frank. **The Role of State Government in the Nineteenth-Century American Economy, 1820-1902:** A Quantitative Study. (Doctoral Dissertation, Purdue University, 1970). 1977

Katz, Harold. **The Decline of Competition in the Automobile Industry, 1920-1940.** (Doctoral Dissertation, Columbia University, 1970). 1977

Lee, Susan Previant. **The Westward Movement of the Cotton Economy, 1840-1860:** Perceived Interests and Economic Realities. (Doctoral Dissertation, Columbia University, 1975). 1977

Legler, John Baxter. **Regional Distribution of Federal Receipts and Expenditures in the Nineteenth Century:** A Quantitative Study. (Doctoral Dissertation, Purdue University, 1967). 1977

Lightner, David L. **Labor on the Illinois Central Railroad, 1852-1900:** The Evolution of an Industrial Environment. (Doctoral Dissertation, Cornell University, 1969). 1977

MacMurray, Robert R. **Technological Change in the American Cotton Spinning Industry, 1790 to 1836.** (Doctoral Dissertation, University of Pennsylvania, 1970). 1977

Netschert, Bruce Carlton. **The Mineral Foreign Trade of the United States in the Twentieth Century:** A Study in Mineral Economics. (Doctoral Dissertation, Cornell University, 1949). 1977

Otenasek, Mildred. **Alexander Hamilton's Financial Policies.** (Doctoral Dissertation, Johns Hopkins University, 1939). 1977

Parks, Robert James. **European Origins of the Economic Ideas of Alexander Hamilton.** (M. A. Thesis, Michigan State University, 1963). 1977

Parsons, Burke Adrian. **British Trade Cycles and American Bank Credit:** Some Aspects of Economic Fluctuations in the United States, 1815-1840. (Doctoral Dissertation, University of Texas, 1958). 1977

Primack, Martin L. **Farm Formed Capital in American Agriculture, 1850-1910.** (Doctoral Dissertation, University of North Carolina, 1963). 1977

Pritchett, Bruce Michael. **A Study of Capital Mobilization, The Life Insurance Industry of the Nineteenth Century.** (Doctoral Dissertation, Purdue University, 1970). Revised Edition. 1977

Prosper, Peter A., Jr. **Concentration and the Rate of Change of Wages in the United States, 1950-1962.** (Doctoral Dissertation, Cornell University 1970). 1977

Schachter, Joseph. **Capital Value and Relative Wage Effects of Immigration into the United States, 1870-1930.** (Doctoral Dissertation, City University of New York, 1969). 1977

Schaefer, Donald Fred. **A Quantitative Description and Analysis of the Growth of the Pennsylvania Anthracite Coal Industry, 1820 to 1865.** (Doctoral Dissertation, University of North Carolina, 1967). 1977

Schmitz, Mark. **Economic Analysis of Antebellum Sugar Plantations in Louisiana.** (Doctoral Dissertation, University of North Carolina, 1974). 1977

Sharpless, John Burk, II. **City Growth in the United States, England and Wales, 1820-1861:** The Effects of Location, Size and Economic Structure on Inter-urban Variations in Demographic Growth. (Doctoral Dissertation, University of Michigan, 1975). 1977

Shields, Roger Elwood. **Economic Growth with Price Deflation, 1873-1896.** (Doctoral Dissertation, University of Virginia, 1969). 1977

Stettler, Henry Louis, III. **Growth and Fluctuations in the Ante-Bellum Textile Industry.** (Doctoral Dissertation, Purdue University, 1970). 1977

Sturm, James Lester. **Investing in the United States, 1798-1893:** Upper Wealth-Holders in a Market Economy. (Doctoral Dissertation, University of Wisconsin, 1969). 1977

Tenenbaum, Marcel. **(A Demographic Analysis of Interstate Labor Growth Rate Differentials;** United States, 1890-1900 to 1940-50. (Doctoral Dissertation, Columbia University, 1969). 1977

Thomas, Robert Paul. **An Analysis of the Pattern of Growth of the Automobile Industry:** 1895-1929. (Doctoral Dissertation, Northwestern University, 1965). 1977

Vickery, William Edward. **The Economics of the Negro Migration 1900-1960.** (Doctoral Dissertation, University of Chicago, 1969). 1977

Waters, Joseph Paul. **Technological Acceleration and the Great Depression.** (Doctoral Dissertation, Cornell University, 1971). 1977

Whartenby, Franklee Gilbert. **Land and Labor Productivity in United States Cotton Production, 1800-1840.** (Doctoral Dissertation, University of North Carolina, 1963). 1977

1975 Publications

Adams, Donald R., Jr. **Wage Rates in Philadelphia, 1790-1830.** (Doctoral Dissertation, University of Pennsylvania, 1967). 1975

Aldrich, Terry Mark. **Rates of Return on Investment in Technical Education in the Ante-Bellum American Economy.** (Doctoral Dissertation, The University of Texas at Austin, 1969). 1975

Anderson, Terry Lee. **The Economic Growth of Seventeenth Century New England:** A Measurement of Regional Income. (Doctoral Dissertation, University of Washington, 1972). 1975

Bean, Richard Nelson. **The British Trans-Atlantic Slave Trade, 1650-1775.** (Doctoral Dissertation, University of Washington, 1971). 1975

Brock, Leslie V. **The Currency of the American Colonies, 1700-1764:** A Study in Colonial Finance and Imperial Relations. (Doctoral Dissertation University of Michigan, 1941). 1975

Ellsworth, Lucius F. **Craft to National Industry in the Nineteenth Century:** A Case Study of the Transformation of the New York State Tanning Industry. (Doctoral Dissertation, University of Delaware, 1971). 1975

Fleisig, Heywood W. **Long Term Capital Flows and the Great Depression:** The Role of the United States, 1927-1933. (Doctoral Dissertation, Yale University, 1969). 1975

Foust, James D. **The Yeoman Farmer and Westward Expansion of U.S. Cotton Production.** (Doctoral Dissertation, University of North Carolina at Chapel Hill, 1968). 1975

Golden, James Reed. **Investment Behavior By United States Railroads, 1870-1914.** (Doctoral Thesis, Harvard University, 1971). 1975

Hill, Peter Jensen. **The Economic Impact of Immigration into the United States.** (Doctoral Dissertation, The University of Chicago, 1970). 1975

Klingaman, David C. **Colonial Virginia's Coastwise and Grain Trade.** (Doctoral Dissertation, University of Virginia, 1967). 1975

Lang, Edith Mae. **The Effects of Net Interregional Migration on Agricultural Income Growth:** The United States, 1850-1860. (Doctoral Thesis, The University of Rochester, 1971). 1975

Lindley, Lester G. **The Constitution Faces Technology:** The Relationship of the National Government to the Telegraph, 1866-1884. (Doctoral Thesis, Rice University, 1971). 1975

Lorant, John H[erman]. **The Role of Capital-Improving Innovations in American Manufacturing During the 1920's.** (Doctoral Thesis, Columbia University, 1966). 1975

Mishkin, David Joel. **The American Colonial Wine Industry:** An Economic Interpretation, Volumes I and II. (Doctoral Thesis, University of Illinois, 1966). 1975

Winkler, Donald R. **The Production of Human Capital:** A Study of Minority Achievement. (Doctoral Dissertation, University of California at Berkeley, 1972). 1977

Oates, Mary J. **The Role of the Cotton Textile Industry in the Economic Development of the American Southeast:** 1900-1940. (Doctoral Dissertation, Yale University, 1969). 1975

Passell, Peter. **Essays in the Economics of Nineteenth Century American Land Policy.** (Doctoral Dissertation, Yale University, 1970). 1975

Pope, Clayne L. **The Impact of the Ante-Bellum Tariff on Income Distribution.** (Doctoral Dissertation, The University of Chicago, 1972). 1975

Poulson, Barry Warren. **Value Added in Manufacturing, Mining, and Agriculture in the American Economy From 1809 To 1839.** (Doctoral Dissertation, The Ohio State University, 1965). 1975

Rockoff, Hugh. **The Free Banking Era: A Re-Examination.** (Doctoral Dissertation, The University of Chicago, 1972). 1975

Schumacher, Max George. **The Northern Farmer and His Markets During the Late Colonial Period.** (Doctoral Dissertation, University of California at Berkeley, 1948). 1975

Seagrave, Charles Edwin. **The Southern Negro Agricultural Worker:** 1850-1870. (Doctoral Dissertation, Stanford University, 1971). 1975

Solmon, Lewis C. **Capital Formation by Expenditures on Formal Education, 1880 and 1890.** (Doctoral Dissertation, The University of Chicago, 1968). 1975

Swan, Dale Evans. **The Structure and Profitability of the Antebellum Rice Industry:** 1859. (Doctoral Dissertation, University of North Carolina at Chapel Hill, 1972). 1975

Sylla, Richard Eugene. **The American Capital Market, 1846-1914:** A Study of the Effects of Public Policy on Economic Development. (Doctoral Thesis, Harvard University, 1968). 1975

Uselding, Paul John. **Studies in the Technological Development of the American Economy During the First Half of the Nineteenth Century.** (Doctoral Dissertation, Northwestern University, 1970). 1975

Walsh, William D[avid]. **The Diffusion of Technological Change in the Pennsylvania Pig Iron Industry, 1850-1870.** (Doctoral Dissertation, Yale University, 1967). 1975

Weiss, Thomas Joseph. **The Service Sector in the United States, 1839 Through 1899.** (Doctoral Thesis, University of North Carolina at Chapel Hill, 1967). 1975

Zevin, Robert Brooke. **The Growth of Manufacturing in Early Nineteenth Century New England.** 1975